VISUAL MERCHANDISING AND STORE DESIGN

WORKBOOK

MERCHANDISING, FIXTURING AND LIGHTING CREATE VISUAL EXCITEMENT FOR RETAIL STORES

by Greg M. Gorman

MEDIA GROUP INTERNATIONAL

Cincinnati, Ohio

Published by ST Media Group International, Inc.

ISBN: 0-944094-20-1
ISBN-13: 978-0-944094-20-4

To contact the publisher:
ST Books
ST Media Group International Inc.
11262 Cornell Park Drive
Cincinnati, Ohio 45242 USA
Tel: 513-263-9399
Fax: 513-744-6999
Email: books@stmediagroup.com
Website: www.bookstore.stmediagroup.com

To contact the author:
Gregory M. Gorman
Email: greg@gmgdesigninc.com
Website: www.gmgdesigninc.com

Book design: Greg M. Norman
Cover design: Carole Winters

Printed in the United States of America

TABLE OF CONTENTS

ABOUT THE AUTHOR

Greg M. Gorman has been involved in creative design since he was a young boy in grade school. He studied art and design throughout both high school and college. With an interest in retail design, he became interested in the store planning and visual merchandising fields. In order to understand the total space and how to communicate with all persons involved with projects, he also studied engineering, architecture, landscaping and graphic communications.

Greg's experiences range from involvement with department and specialty store design to vendor shops. He started his own company GMG DESIGN, in 1992. His clients have ranged from those listed above directly, through fixture manufacturers, to architectural firms and designers of corporate identity programs. He has developed a seminar program on Store Design and Visual Merchandising which has been presented at many different tradeshows and conventions. He understands merchandising and is capable of working any types of merchandise requirements.

Before starting his own company, Greg worked for major corporations in both better-grade and value-priced environments. His well-rounded exposures and love for retail design are the main reasons he started his own firm.

As an educator at a local community college in Saint Louis he is able to expose and interest others in the field of retail store design. He is also very active as the Fundraising Chairman of PAVE, The Planning and Visual Education Partnership; and ISP, The Institute of Store Planners. Both of these organizations have strong educational commitments to the fields through students.

Greg's main interest in retail design is focused on the smaller retailers. He has designed specialty stores in malls and street locations from coast to coast, in South America and on the water through a cruise ship client. Through product manufacturers, vendor shops and creative and visual merchandising support for architectural firms, he has effected great changes in many middle-sized and larger retail names.

FOREWORD

Many store design projects start with the architect developing a space and turning over the finished box to the retailer or owner. My approach to store design is not as heavily weighted to architecturally permanent design elements. These items are generally approached through fixtures or other means of visual excitement in the store. When based on less permanence and greater mobility and flexibility, the retailer can greater accept and work with changes in merchandise and trends. It also allows for different allocation in prioritizing the budget.

The only way to start a store design concept is to fully understand the merchandise. Once that is defined, it is time to focus on the customer, location demographically as well as specific location and overall store identity or image. Once defined, the real FUN begins with adding great merchandising and what I call Visual Excitement. The visual excitement is what supports and in many situations becomes the store image and identity which the customer is exposed to from a total shopping environment experience. Remember, it has to start with the merchandise.

The purpose of this book, workbook, tool, is to introduce the concept of store design from a design direction. It is intended for students and store owners. It allows the reader to fully understand all aspects of the retail store requirements and how they all have an effect on the final product, the store. The tool has been strongly influenced by three major elements which are best defined as Visual Excitement. They can also at times be referenced as Retail Theatre. The three areas are MERCHANDISING, which covers general presentation and visual support, FIXTURING, and LIGHTING.

The small retailer typically doesn't have the larger budgets for either new or remodel construction. He must be focused tighter on every element included in the store. At the same time he is competing with major retailers who allocate yearly budgets for fixtures, signage, lighting, etc., and employ persons responsible to produce programs for new products, trends and simply aesthetic change. Therefore, the smaller retailer must know where and how to best invest in the future to compete.

It is easily achieved through proper allocation and planning for smaller retailers to create excitement and attract customers into their stores. It is easily achieved with smaller budgets. However, a plan needs to be developed to accommodate change on an on-going basis. For example, in a particular store, the owner locates a focal fixture unit directly inside the store entrance as the first element the customer views. This fixture is capable of accepting and displaying many different types and sizes of merchandise, thus being totally flexible. It also has some individual personality through detail, finishes and size that is more fixture intense than merchandise intense. This fixture is actually a center freestanding focal point. It immediately stops the customer and introduces both product and store image.

This fixture is the start of a fixture program and development of overall store image. The next step is to add other points of interest on the side and rear wall areas. These focal points are either within the merchandise area, typically up to 84" or above. When above, and merchandise is not against the ceiling line, this raise in merchandising and visual excitement attracts the eye of customers. Fixturing can be freestanding on the floor or wall standards with shelves having some interest, painted or applied finish changes, merchandised or graphic additions. There are many applicable possibilities and options available.

Since change is a consistent factor, make sure that whenever you merchandise focal areas or add dimensional visual support, that it is rotated on a regular basis. This will allow the store to always appear new and fresh. Visual props and displays can at times play a major role in adding to the visual excitement. Graphics and signage work well as background and support for a theme or merchandise selection.

Once the focal points are established and completed, lighting is required to further draw attention to the areas. The light will attract the eyes of the customer and move them toward certain parts of the store.

Although smaller retailers do not always have the larger budgets, they are often better positioned to effect change in their stores. The reason for this is that, once a decision is made to change an area with new elements, through fixtures, etc., smaller retailers don't have to make presentations and gain approvals before things can happen. Since the owner most times is involved with the designs and decisions, change happens immediately. Obtaining products is also made easier since items can be purchased or made locally. This ability to quickly respond is one of the greatest assets to small retailers.

The owners of smaller businesses typically also work in the store or stores daily. They are more willing to work with a customer to satisfy their individual needs. The owners want the customer to return and even tell their friends through word of mouth advertising about the store. The owner to customer rapport found in small businesses, that personal touch, is priceless.

Smaller retailers often get into a particular type of business due to a love or passion for the merchandise type or direction. They are truly experts in the related products offered as opposed to simply sales or stock clerks. Larger retailers often tend to ignore or underestimate this aspect of service.

It is also important to note that local merchants live in the areas of their customers. Their children attend the same schools and play on the same little league sports teams. Smaller retailers are often involved through support and endorsements with local community events. This shows the customers and potential customers that they truly are dedicated to the area. Even though the small retailer may not be able to offer the same low prices, since they are often closer and respected as part of the community, the customers are also loyal in return.

Note that price alone is not the only factor involved in a sale. Making sales and purchases entail many other factors.

It is strongly urged for all retailers to not only understand their customers but also the competition. Regular visits to other stores should be scheduled. Look at their interior environments, and determine what stands out or doesn't. Evaluate and compare with your stores or others and determine how to develop a different look and feel. Don't copy directly, introduce newness. Many major retailers simply copy each other and what happens is they all start to look alike. The customer notices these aspects even though upper management may simply want to copy something based on someone else's success. Always offer new.

If you are not comfortable with certain aspects of retail store design simply ask questions of others. If necessary employ the services of professionals in the related fields of need. Call upon manufacturers' sales representatives to understand new trends. Work with schools in the area. The importance of including all the different aspects of store design in this book is to at least make the reader aware of where and when outside support is required.

Communication is so important between stores and customers. It is amazing how much a store owner can learn from the customers. Ask them questions regarding merchandise, price and overall store environments. Where else do they shop and why? Start mailing lists and constantly send information to customers.

Retail can be both fun and brutal. It takes a very special type of person to be involved with retail and all the different aspects of the industry. However, retail can be a lot of fun and very rewarding. It takes constant attention and change to stay ahead and offer the best.

Whenever possible, retailers and designers alike should attend conventions and tradeshows. These bring exposure to merchandising trends, resources and presentation directions. Many times there are seminars that apply to your needs sponsored at conventions. Attendance at seminars allows the attendee to be exposed to new ideas or receive support for existing practices through reinforcement by others. You can learn a little or a lot from a seminar. A little can go long way if properly applied to your specific need. The other important thing to remember is that while you may not require information today on a certain aspect of retailing, you may need it tomorrow.

CHANGE

No matter how you find it defined, change is the most important part of a successful retail story.

Everything changes and has an effect on your store, your customers, their spending habits and the time they dedicate to shopping. In order to survive, you must change accordingly.

To fight change is to admit defeat and successful retailers don't get out of bed each day and subject themselves to working long hours to be defeated. Instead, each day they listen to their customers, learn about new trends, the latest products, new means of fixturing and merchandising their stores, and prepare to reap the benefits that will follow. They expose themselves to the latest in technological issues and tools. It's their job to be educated and to educate.

Yes, it's a retailer's job to educate the customer and introduce them to new ideas. Retailers must educate and grow their own sales associates so that they can do the same when representing the store image. The customer isn't always open to all changes immediately. Be patient with them and with yourself.

But some things shouldn't change if they are still appropriate. For example, you wouldn't cut your sales staff in half if you are known and recognized for having knowledgeable sales associates. You shouldn't start to carry lower-priced merchandise just because your competition does. Remember, you must stay focused on what already works well in your business. You mustn't change just for the sake of change.

As a small retailer, the entrepreneurial behavior is typically more evident. So, make change happen for your store and don't wait. Since you understand your business and trends, try new ideas on a regular basis. Conduct little tests and weigh the results either through increased sales, traffic through the store, etc.

Expose yourself to anything and everything that can be applied to your particular business. As a designer in retail design, the same should apply. Read trade magazines to understand directions, trends, resources, finishes and materials and who is doing what. There is a lot to learn from catalogs where, in a different sense, retailers have included visual excitement within to support products. Even viewing of cable shopping networks will illustrate to you the importance of certain aspects of selling.

DEFINE YOUR CUSTOMER

It is impossible to own and operate a business without having and knowing a target customer.

You also must define the exact direction you want to go with and grow with your customer. Don't try to be everything to everyone. Determine a direction plan and stick with it. Don't give up on the plan if at first it appears not to be working for you. Give it a fair chance to succeed before you consider it doomed. Continually critique your plan and look for ways to improve it.

WHO IS YOUR TARGET CUSTOMER?

STAY FOCUSED ON THEM. DON'T STRAY UNLESS IT IS NECESSARY AS PART OF AN OVERALL REALIGNMENT PLAN.

Fill in the list of customer descriptives below adding others if necessary:

Sex _____ Ethnic Group _____ Age Group _____
Family Oriented _____ Married or Single _____
Adults _____ Children _____ Profession/Occupation _____
Yearly Household Income _____
Own Home or Rent _____ City or Suburban _____
Lifestyle _____
Hobbies _____

Where do they typically shop and how often:
Outlet Stores _____ Home Shopping Networks _____
Outlet Malls _____ Catalogs _____
Regional Malls _____ Discount Stores _____
Department Stores _____ Warehouse Clubs _____

Strip Centers _____ Garage Sales _____
Specialty Stores _____
Average Purchase Amount _____
Cash or Credit _____

In retail, the customer is the most important aspect of the business next to proper merchandise. Yet at the same time, the customer is always changing based on possible expendable income, relocation and needs.

When designing a store, it is always important to understand the target customer. Far too often the design concept is based on the likes and dislikes of the owner or store designer. This and other aspects should always be based on the prospective customer.

Demographically speaking, make sure that your store is located where the target customer is or frequents. Remembering that convenience is an important aspect of the success formula.

When advertising is utilized, make sure the message is targeted to the customer. And of course, advertise where your customer reads or on radio stations that they listen to regularly. Although not every retailer is able to utilize cable television, don't underestimate the importance of cable and regular television advertisements. Local stations are always willing to work with smaller local retailers, for they too are trying to survive in the community.

Whenever in doubt, talk with your customers. They are usually truthful and willing to explain opinions on what they like and dislike. Listen to what they say or what their body language says when they are in your store. Many retailers develop short questionnaires for the customer to answer regarding the store. Consider everything they say as a possibility for improvement.

IDENTIFY YOUR COMPETITION

"Keep your friends close, but your ENEMIES closer."

While this harsh statement was made by Michael Corleone in "The Godfather," there's a serious message in it for retailers. We must never fail to recognize and remember our competition. Your competition is going after the same customer as you are on a daily basis. To be successful in retailing you must be able to accurately identify your competition. Be realistic, but at the same time stretch it a bit. You don't want to miss anyone. The list may be long. Set it aside for a while, then take another look at it, and eliminate the superfluous ones.

Then ask yourself some questions:

What is your competition doing differently from you this week?

What did they do differently last week, or month?

What are their best sellers? And what is the regular price and the promotional price?

What do they do differently with their in-store displays, windows, walls and sales floor?

How often do they change their displays?

What is their marketing/promotional material and how often is it sent to customers?

What new product are they trying? What worked, what failed?

The list goes on — make sure you frequently visit their stores and know their businesses.

When making the list of competitors, never underestimate anyone or anything. It is not always possible to understand exactly what attracts the customer although some things are more obvious than others.

Your list should start with "like retail businesses" in the immediate area where your store is located. Like businesses sell basically the same lines of merchandise. However, there will be some retailers that carry other lines as well, depending on their focus or size of store. Department and discount stores will drive items for resale. Specialty and franchise operations will generally be focused tighter and may be able to influence the customer with prices also.

Don't underestimate catalogs and cable TV home shopping networks. There are many customers that simply don't enjoy shopping all the time or physically cannot and will purchase from these media opportunities. When time is a factor, these two can be strong competitors.

It is possible to learn about your competition through your actual customers. After all, if your customers do purchase from your competition or frequent their stores it is for a specific reason. Even if your customers don't shop at some of your competitors, understand why.

Many times I explain to clients and retailers in general that they need to open their minds and entertain many options. When researching for retail comparisons, do's and don'ts, consider stores that are completely opposite of what you sell or are designing towards. Over the years, clothing or softlines retailing has spent more money on research and development than most other merchandise categories. With an open mind and wanting to be different than your competition, discover new approaches to merchandising. Find an exciting fixture or display focal point and then imagine your particular product offerings on the unit. Use your imagination and don't be afraid of failure.

IDENTIFY YOUR WEAKNESSES AND STRENGTHS

Once you have become intimate with your competition, then you must rationally and critically analyze your own operation. How does it compare to that of your competitors?

Focus on your strengths and look for ways to improve. Then, focus on your weaknesses now and define new ways to correct serious mistakes. If being constructively critical about your own business is difficult, then ask someone else to honestly evaluate your business for you. As long as the approach is constructive and honest, you can at least accept it as another opinion, right or wrong.

Walk through the front door of your store and pretend you are the customer. Ask yourself:

What immediately stands out first? Where is it? Is it a positive or negative feeling?

What overall store image and personality are being conveyed through merchandise, decor, fixturing and point-of-sale signage?

Is your store visually easy to understand and shop?

What type of customer would enter your store based on what you see and feel initially?

Where are the sales associates? Where's the cashwrap counter?

Can you easily identify the name of the store you just walked into?

What's the lighting like? Does it complement the merchandising on the walls and sales floor? Are there highlighted areas attracting you to specific parts within the store?

Remember that you are in business to meet the needs of your customers. Many times it is necessary to disregard personal likes and dislikes to meet the customers' needs.

If there are items that require modification, try testing new approaches and evaluate the results. Don't become your own worst enemy by simply ignoring advice and customer signals.

Keep in mind that not everyone is a expert in all areas of retailing and outside advice is necessary. There is a lot to be learned from magazine articles, books and videotapes. Most communities have frequent programs designed for retailers and more specifically to meet the needs of retailers.

If talking or meeting with others to discuss your particular situation is uncomfortable for you, try surfing the internet for applicable solutions.

COMMUNITY INVOLVEMENT

Involvement in the community is a wonderful practice and a good marketing/advertising tool. Not only does it establish you as a concerned citizen but evokes certain loyalty from the community.

There are many ways to become involved:
- Donations directly to charities and organizations
- Sponsorship of team sports
- Discounts to community organizations
- Contests at various holidays
- Selling of merchandise manufactured in your community and state
- Advertisements in local papers
- Involvement with local schools

Take a look at the community you serve and imagine the opportunities that exist for you and your store. Remember, when you directly involve your store and customers, traffic increases. For example, sponsor a poster or window painting contest with a school and display the entries. Contestants will bring friends and family to view the competition. The exposure is priceless.

You may want to offer internships for students to understand how to run a small business. The interns may even be paid minimum wage for actual hours or make it part of a class credit program. Limit the internships to a few weeks or a month and involve greater numbers of students. You may be surprised that the students can even teach you something!

SALES ASSOCIATES MOTIVATION

Working in a positive environment is crucial to having a successful store. Regardless of staff size, there's always going to be something that slows progress every now and then. In order to maintain a positive work environment, you as the owner/manager must be aware of frustration when it first hits — before it gets out of control.

Listed are a few suggestions. If all else fails, there are many professionals in business management and staffing who can lend support through personal consultation, suggested readings or even seminars to your entire organization.

- Observe behaviors during work and on breaks
- Take note of individual tastes
- Encourage good work; reinforcing superior job performances goes a long way toward improving the quality of the work environment
- Make notes about the response and results to the reward; different people require different reinforcers
- Ask your staff what makes them excited and act accordingly; paid time off is always a sure winner
- Make sure that you reinforce the right behavior
- Reinforce often

You may want to create games that accumulate points to be cashed in for prizes, cash incentives or even vacation time. Let your associates be a part of decision making and reap the benefits of success as well. Such ownership increases personal commitment. Not only that, two heads are often better than one.

- Be a team player.
- Be a partner
- Make it FUN!!!
- Don't forget to say, "Thank you."

CUSTOMER SERVICE

"THE CUSTOMER IS ALWAYS RIGHT."

Everybody recognizes this phrase, but not everyone accepts it as the truth. The fact is, as retailers, your are dependent on the customer and the opinion they have about your store. Not just the merchandise but the attitude and courtesy of the sales associates. The knowledge sales associates have regarding the merchandise and services available in the store is important as well.

"A smile goes a long way."
"It takes more muscles to frown than it does to smile."
"Common courtesy makes common sense."

Often the sales associate is so the first and last impression that a customer has of your store. Make sure it is a positive one. Sales associates should always practice courtesy and respect when it comes to the customer. The sales staff's role is really to meet the needs of the customer and help to make the shopping experience as enjoyable as possible. Granted, based on all the different personalities in this world, some interactions are better than others. Treat the customer as you wish to be treated — with respect.

One of the most important things to do is to thank customers for stopping in your store even if they didn't purchase anything at the time. They may return at a different time and make a purchase.

The retailer may also offer service related programs such as :
• Layaway
• Free packaging or shipping
• Consultant services relating to their products
• Repairs and warranties
• Credit programs
• Custom design and manufacturing

Be creative when it comes to services made available to the customers. Develop programs that will differentiate you from other retailers.

I was working with a particular client, a retailer that does quite a bit of seasonal business similar to outlet malls. Their customers came from all across the country making yearly visits to the store. This was true commitment. They are also a regular stop with bus trips and shopping tours. They had a guest book asking for comments and their names. However, they did not request an address. The book was changed requesting this information and now they have a very extensive mailing list of first-time and loyal customers. This list can be used to advertise great products and prices along with simply sending a seasonal hello.

Another client with a bookstore started a reading club with benefits based on a certain amount of books purchased. This is similar to coffee cafes that award a free cup when a certain amount of coffee is consumed. The list and stories go on and on. The main point to remember is that those with entrepreneurial spirit are constantly thinking of new ways to differentiate themselves from their competition.

Holding past jobs with small retailers and major corporations, I realize that store-level moral at times can drop to all time lows. Try to keep yourself as store owners aware of such swings. One proven way to keep employees excited is to make them a part of the entire retail experience. Create games and contests involving them in successful retailing. Ask them questions, their opinions and reward them when they contribute in a positive way to the growth and success of the store.

You will find that there are typically various management seminars and lectures that can be attended for free or at a minimal fee in your community. Check with local colleges and schools or even small business organizations. Many books are available on the market and if that doesn't work, then buy or rent motivational tapes.

Don't let others negatively control your destiny. Stop them. Work toward correcting the situation if possible. If that doesn't work, replace them. However, look for the right person as a replacement, not just the first through the door. People-management skills are not always easily obtained and sometimes require daily attention. Remember to consider others and work with them. Accept them as a part of the team and they will in return, most times, reward you with a great work environment full of positive attitudes and smiles.

HOW TO BUDGET FOR YOUR STORE

No matter how great the overall store design is, if it exceeds the anticipated budget amount it may not work. At the same time, it is not always easy to determine exactly what all the actual costs involved will be.

However, you have to start somewhere and a cost estimate must be developed. Working together as a team, client and designer should discuss the budget, define all important components of the finished store and estimate dollars accordingly. There are general costs that can be used for many areas but with so many options and changing materials, they do not always apply.

The best way to start is to estimate slightly higher than actual to be safe at the end. Keep in mind that with the cost estimate, anything can be changed prior to start of actual services or purchases and installation.

Start by making a list of all anticipated items that will be necessary to complete the project. When making the list you must start to define certain design aspects and operational issues of the project. All parties involved will also begin to better under- stand each other and apply all newly found information to the project. If you know in advance that certain resources like the general contractor, fixture manufacturer, etc., are involved, ask them to attend the initial meeting. The greater the communication between all parties, the better the flow of the project and more accurate end results.

The list should include as much as possible:

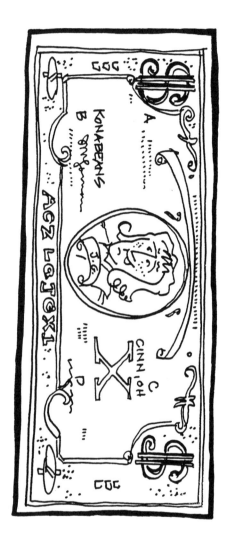

MATERIALS	SERVICES	RESPONSIBLE COSTS
----------	Design	$
Flooring	Purchase	$
	Installation	$
Wall Coverings	Purchase	$
	Installation	$
Lighting	Design	$
	Purchase	$
	Installation	$
Ceiling	Design	$
	Purchase	$
	Installation	$
Sales Floor Fixtures	Design	$
	Purchase	$
	Installation	$
Stock Room Fixtures	Purchase	$
	Installation	$
Office Equipment	Purchase	$
	Installation	$
Fixture Hardware	Design	$
	Purchase	$
	Installation	$
Graphics	Design	$
	Purchase	$
	Installation	$
Signage	Design	$
	Purchase	$
	Installation	$
Signholders	Design	$
	Purchase	$
	Installation	$

Visual Displays and Props	Design	$
	Purchase	$
	Installation	$
Exterior Lighting	Design	$
	Purchase	$
	Installation	$
Ext. Arch. Elements	Design	$
	Purchase	$
	Installation	$
Lighting	Design	$
	Purchase	$
	Installation	$
Canopies	Design	$
	Purchase	$
	Installation	$
Security/Alarms	Purchase	$
	Installation	$
Sound System	Purchase	$
	Installation	$
Demolition		$
New Construction		$
Trash Removal		$
Clean Up		$
Plumbing		$
HVAC		$
Phone		$
Estimated tax and freight as applicable		$
Sub-Total		$

Add 10% $

Grand Total $

Keep in mind that this list may not cover everything but should greatly assist with the initial budget estimation.

When designing and building the first of several stores with the same design concept, the first will always be higher if all conditions are the same. This is because the first is considered the prototype and refinement, value engineering, new resourcing, etc., will tend to happen with additional stores. Changes are typical also since things change as well as tastes, trends, products and so on.

PROFESSIONAL DESIGN SERVICES

Once the decision has been made to open a new store, the process begins with the search for a designer. You should be careful in your selection and look for several different and important items.

First, start with someone who is experienced in retail store design which includes years of experience in merchandising. Many owners start with an architect for the design and development of a store and receive acceptable spaces. However, without the merchandising experience, it will not typically work as desired. It is not to say that architects are not capable of such a task. But it is typically not what they have been educated in to provide nor do they experience it on a daily basis.

Some design firms have combined the experiences of architects, merchandisers and draftsmen. However, the larger the firm, the larger the overhead. The larger the overhead, the greater the design service fee that is passed onto the client. Smaller design firms do exist that specialize with small retail clients as opposed to the search for major corporations with deeper pockets. Smaller firms are generally more in touch with the realities of smaller retailers on a daily basis.

When choosing a firm or firms, the place to start is interviews and portfolio review of past projects. You should ask to review past or current projects that best align themselves with your particular needs. Retail store designers must wear many hats. As mentioned earlier, they must understand merchandising. This is where it all begins and evolves around, start to finish. They must also understand basic code requirements and how to work with them to incur minimal costs and not just simply specify typical standards which yield higher costs. That is because it is easier to simply specify than to investigate ways around certain rules and regulations that do not always apply to smaller retail operations.

Also keep in mind that if the particular project requires support above and beyond the normal services, a smaller firm is apt to hire such services. It is important to understand that firms of all sizes, even larger ones, do not always have all services under one roof. This is smart business if you are not in need of such services on a regular basis.

Once you have chosen a particular design firm it is necessary to discuss design fees, timing, etc. I usually start with a short questionnaire that is completed by the client. So often the client wants to know what the costs will be up front without preliminary discussion just to get an idea. Since projects vary from each other it is nearly impossible to estimate design services and applicable fees without detailed information.

When the preliminary form is completed and returned, the cost estimation begins. Keep in mind that this beginning, first, contract proposal can be modified if it is not exactly what each party, the store owner (client in this example) and design firm are comfortable with to initiate the relationship.

While there are standard forms that can be used as the contract, I have found that each particular project should be approached individually. That means the form must be personalized to meet the specific needs of the client in each situation.

It is recommended to never work without a contract which is agreed upon by both/all parties involved. The contract will or should define all important aspects of the services and project. It serves as protection for both parties in the event that one of the parties doesn't fulfill its commitment with the project.

The contract is set-up in certain parts as listed:

1. DEFINITION OF ALL PARTIES INVOLVED WITH THE PROJECT
It is very possible that the actual project may involve more than simply the client/store owner and design firm. It is at times common to work with merchandisers specialized in certain fields, separate engineers, architects and general contractors. When each may have a particular role, each role must be defined.

It is also very important to define the actual contact person within the clients office to avoid confusion with who requested what.

For example, I recently worked with a medium-sized corporation designing a new store concept that could have roll-out potential. The in-house contacts were defined and worked with on a daily basis during all of the planning stages of the project. When it came time for the first installation, someone outside of the originally defined in-house contacts got involved and did not consult with the previous defined contacts. The results could have been a nightmare if there wasn't a very defined and detailed contract for design services. It was also valuable to have documentation of all decisions and requests throughout the extent of the project in the file. The newly assigned contact looked at certain aspects of merchandising differently from the original team. When the person wasn't happy with the first prototype and made certain requests for changes, the contract served as the final ruling on who was responsible for what services. The final result was that the actual general contractor was found to be in error along with his chosen fixture manufacturer and not the design firm.

2. DEFINED SCOPE OF SERVICES TO BE PERFORMED
Detailed definition of the actual services needs to be indicated in the contract in order to include all of the client's requests and to exclude anything that is felt unnecessary. This portion defines the actual design services and creative portion of the project.

3. TIMING AND ACTION SCHEDULE
Verification of expected completion date is absolutely necessary in the contract. This portion defines the stages of the entire project with dates. (See the sample Timing and Action Schedule on page 38.)

4. PROFESSIONAL DESIGN FEES
This portion can be handled in many different ways but should include estimated hours, all inclusions effecting costs and all exclusions not included.

It may be that the costs are definite, or estimated and allowing for additional fees if certain aspects change during the course of the project. Since time is money, design firms must estimate hours but cannot afford to greatly exceed the estimate based on changes or extra added requests from the client.

5. CONCEPT DESIGN OWNERSHIP

This area in the contract usually states that the design firm cannot use the finished concept for other clients but can use it for marketing purposes in the future.

6. CONFIDENTIALITY CLAUSE

It is important to let the client know that any business and facts discussed as necessary to provide services will not be discussed with other outside parties. It is also important at times for the design firm to be protected against others knowing fees involved since each project is so, or can be, different.

7. REIMBURSABLES

In addition to the design fees there are typically items involved to include travel, phone and fax services, postage, sample purchases, lodging, etc., that are unknown at time of initial contract approval. The design firm must protect itself against major expenses incurred as deemed necessary by the client.

8. CHANGES TO CONTRACT

Any and all changes to the issued contract for approval by both parties must be made in writing and approved by signatures.

9. CANCELLATION OF CONTRACT

In case of one party's failure to perform accordingly as stated in the contract, there must be a way to cancel the contract safely for everyone involved.

10. PAYMENT TERMS

This portion defines exactly when the client is required to pay the design firm. It may actually state amounts and days to receive payment.

The design firm should send invoices at each stage of the project as defined to ensure proper and prompt payment.

11. ACCEPTANCE OF CONTRACT

A down payment is required to start the design process from the client. No work starts until receipt of the first payment. Signatures by both parties and dates are also required to finalize the arrangement.

Again, not all contracts are exactly the same. Some may be shorter than this example and others may be longer to include certain aspects deemed necessary.

Many store owners feel it is extremely necessary to work with a designer in their own state or even community. This is not true to receive professional and complete services. With a knowledge of retail store design, long distance relationships work just fine. Travel is completed as required and many times only at the beginning and end of the project. Information can be easily transmitted and understood via phone, fax and delivery services such as UPS, Federal Express or DHL.

I have found at times that local projects often increase the time commitment since personal meetings are expected by the client. Remember, your time is money.

Just the opposite, I have worked with clients in other countries who cannot speak English, nor I their language. After the initial meeting, information was sent by fax and postage, translated as required, supported with photos and videotapes for a complete understanding of the construction and completion processes. It also helps that I am capable of actually defining my design intent quickly with sketches. I can draw and design in any language. A picture can truly be worth a thousand words.

CONTRACT PROPOSAL FOR STORE DESIGN AND MARKETING PACKAGE PREPARED BY GMG DESIGN FOR _____

The purpose of this proposal is to identify all important aspects of the design package and associated design fees required to complete. Please review the following pages and discuss any/all portions as required enabling you to completely understand the proposal.

SCOPE OF SERVICES

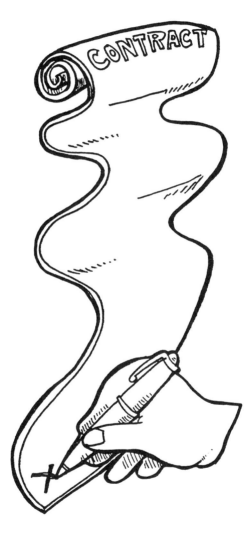

GMG DESIGN (GMG) will provide services to complete this project based on the request of _____, _____. Outlined and listed in the following are the identified necessary areas of importance concerning which GMG will deliver a complete store design package. In addition, there is reference to a marketing package required to identify _____ and the new imaging to existing and new customers, and possibly as a franchise opportunity.

GMG will provide the following services:

• Initial review and critique of existing retail and manufacturing plants in _____, _____ for the purpose of determining a new store design direction. The direct application is for the new store location in the Factory Shops of _____. The completion and grand opening date is August, 1996.

Estimated hours to complete this portion is 16.

• Provide initial design roughs in reference to definition of store space. This will be achieved through block plans, space planning, traffic flow and merchandise adjacencies. Interior design concept will start to be defined and identified in this portion through rough sketches. Initial design development will include interior elevations, perspectives, graphics and signage, fixture design, some finishes and lighting indication. This will be the first exposure to the actual overall store design imaging with application to the new mall location.

Information on the new store location will need to be provided to GMG from _____ in order to completely understand the location opportunities, restrictions, landlord requirements, local city requirements and restrictions.

Estimated hours to complete the initial rough design phase is 74.

• Fixture design definition and detailing for review, approval, merchandising direction for standard areas and specified key focals within the store, finish and material specifications, resourcing for competitive pricing, evaluation of resources for application.

Estimated hours to complete this portion is 67.

• Finalization of actual concept in scaled design package for actual general contractor review, mall/landlord approval, construction and code approvals. Coordination with architects.

Estimated hours to complete this portion is 47.

• Merchandise presentation and visual merchandising proposal programs to standard areas and defined focals complete with signage application, seasonal changes and display props.

Estimated hours to complete this portion is 40.

It is important to note that communication during all phases of the design process listed will be between GMG, _____, landlord, landlord architect/tenant coordinator, possibly local authorities, general contractor if chosen in advance of completed plans package, resources specified and others as deemed necessary by pertinent parties involved. Open lines of communication are vital to delivery of a complete and successful store design package.

This defined portion of the project is inclusive of all important parts of the total store design.

SUB-TOTAL OF ESTIMATED HOURS REQUIRED TO COMPLETE THIS PORTION IS 244.

• In addition to the first part of the store design proposal package was mention of the opportunity to create a marketing package to identify the new store direction and image. This marketing tool developed can also be utilized as an introduction to potential investors or franchise commitments in other cities and states. The marketing package will include all past information as well as the new store design package. Review of all existing information is necessary for proper overall evaluation and formation of new plans and ideas.

After review of existing materials, GMG will design and format a new package, provide prototypes on several concepts, provide all camera-ready art for production, all specifications, etc.

Estimated hours to complete this portion is 36.

The two parts outlined and defined up to this point are intended to explain all important aspects of the store design and marketing requirements start to finish.

GMG will better define in greater detail any or all areas if required for _____ to fully understand the process and final package.

TOTAL ESTIMATED HOURS FOR BOTH PARTS IS 280.

TRAVEL REQUIREMENTS

It will be necessary for GMG to travel and meet personally with _____
during certain parts of the design process. Those parts are as listed below.

• Initial design contract proposal presentation and review. (1) day

• Presentation of initial design package direction to _____ complete with boards and all pertinent information. (1) day

• Initial meeting with _____ and chosen general contractor to discuss the project, on actual job site prior to any development. This will allow for an extensive question and answer session eliminating any potential confusion and future problems. (1) day

• Job site review during construction to evaluate progress and any potential change orders. (1) day

• Review of actual store just prior to completion to critique and assist with last minute revisions and merchandising needs. This trip would also be an evaluation of the actual store design and marketing. May be in conjunction with the actual center/mall grand opening event. (2-3) days

TIMING AND ACTION SCHEDULE (See page 38 for an example.)

In order to determine the actual Timing and Action Schedule, it is necessary to have further conversation with _____. Once the actual grand opening date is determined by _____, GMG will establish a rough draft for review by _____ and approval by _____. The rough draft is intended to establish the project in terms of weeks and months, start to finish. It will be important to include the general contractor in the final establishment of the schedule. The actual finished schedule will be an estimate and actual dates may vary slightly without a negative effect on the grand opening.

CONFIDENTIALITY CLAUSE

For the interest of both GMG and _____, this project will not be discussed by GMG with anyone who could be a possible competitor. All parts of conversation regarding _____ finances, yearly business, merchandise selection, or other personal business aspects will not be mentioned to anyone by GMG. It is therefore understood from acceptance of contract that all conversations regarding this project will be held in strict confidence between GMG and

_____.

REIMBURSABLES

In addition to the actual design fees, there are items that will need to covered as reimbursables between GMG and _____. _____ will be responsible for reimbursement directly to GMG as defined in the area noted as Payment Terms of this contract.

Reimbursables are items above and beyond the standard design requirements and are defined as listed below:

• Travel, postage, faxes, phone calls, presentation materials, photography, printing, sample securement, camera-ready art and color copies. Travel includes airfare, airport parking, ground transportation in city of destination, and lodging.

PAYMENT TERMS

Design fees are to be paid in three parts. The first part is at acceptance of signed, delivered contract by _____ to GMG. The second part is at the halfway point of the project with the final payment to be made upon delivery of the final package items as defined in the Timing and Action Schedule. This payment definition pertains to all design fees in relation to the Scope of Services listed in this contract.

Travel and reimbursables are to be paid at the end of each month during the extent of this project as based on the Timing and Action Schedule.

GMG will issue both faxes and mailed copies of invoices to support payment terms to be paid within ten days after receipt by _____. Payment to be made in US dollars in full as indicated on the invoices.

CONCEPT DESIGN OWNERSHIP

The complete design concept is the property of _____. However, GMG is entitled to use the completed design concept in both written and photographic means to market GMG services to other clients after completion of said project.

GMG is to be credited for the design concept when mentioned and used in print or photographic means through articles or contests.

GMG will not use in its entirety or similar application any items inherent to the designed and applied imaging of the _____ store design concept with other design projects or clients.

CHANGES TO CONTRACT

Any and all changes to this contract proposal must be submitted in written format and signed by both parties involved, GMG and _____. Signatures by both parties are in agreement to include such changes into the overall contract. Each party must either agree to sign or agree not to sign such changes within forty-eight hours of receipt of the written changes. Faxed copies are to be considered both legal and binding. Original copies will be sent upon request.

CANCELLATION OF CONTRACT

Cancellation of contract by _____ must be handled in the following manner only. A written letter must be sent by certified mail outlining the cancellation intent and reasons for such a request. GMG will have one full week, seven days after receipt of notice to respond accordingly. _____ will be invoiced for all completed work to date at time of final acceptance by GMG. This amount in mention will be submitted along with all other pertinent amounts due per the contract agreement. Upon cancellation, _____ must make the final payment within ten days after receipt of invoice.

ACCEPTANCE OF CONTRACT

Acceptance of contract is approved when each party involved, GMG and _____ sign, date and send, at least by fax, a copy to each party for reference and files. Acceptance is both legal and binding based on signatures and dates on the final page of this contract. A faxed copy will be considered both legal and binding.

DESIGN FEES

GMG has established standard design fees as compared to established design fees in retail design. The standard hourly rate based on the retail design professionals within the industry is $_____-_____. This rate is adopted for use for most clients by GMG based on the full scope of the project and potential long-term relationships.

However, based on the scope of services and potential application of this project for major marketing purposes and if _____ commits to building of all approved design directions without change except through GMG, GMG will consider a reduced hourly rate of $_____ per hour for _____ on this project.

This reduced hourly rate ensures GMG the right as agreed upon by _____ to maintain design integrity on first store in the _____ and all other installations for the first three years after completion of this store.

This reduced rate also guarantees that GMG will be given design recognition at all times in marketing, press releases, industry periodicals, design competitions, etc. It is understood that GMG doesn't own the design concept, simply recognition.

Listed below are the estimated hours and applied design fees:

Part One — Design concept development, 244 hours $_____

Part Two — Marketing package, 36 hours $_____

TOTAL $_____

It is important to note that the reimbursables are in additions to the design fees listed above. Design fees and reimbursables do not cover extra expenses incurred by local code requirements for engineering calculations on energy in regards to lighting, HVAC, permits, licenses, application fees and architectural seals.

Design fees are for the total project design package, both the interior and exterior along with the marketing package.

SIGNATURES AND DATES

When both parties involved in this design proposal sign and date as outlined below, the parties agree to uphold the contents of this contractual agreement.

Both parties have read the pages of this contract and agree with all listed terms unless there is an added page also to be considered part of this contract.

_____   _____

_____   Greg M. Gorman
_____   President
_____   GMG Design
_____   3368 A Oxford Ave.
_____   St. Louis, MO 63143
_____   P 314.644.2590
_____   F 314.644.2591

_____   _____

Date   Date

TIMING AND ACTION SCHEDULE

ACTION/DESCRIPTION	DATES
Approval of design contract	8.28.95
Preliminary design development for actual structure for landlord use and approval (1 week)	8.29.95 - 9.5.95
Landlord approval and possible changes (2 weeks)	9.6.95 - 9.20.95
Design development for signage, interior, plans, etc. (4 weeks)	9.21.95 - 10.12.95
Approval, resourcing needs and finalizing prices (2 weeks)	10.13.95 - 10.26.95
Fixture fabrication and delivery to job site (8 weeks)	10.27.95 - 12.22.95
Installation to completion (1 week)	12.23.95 - 12.30.95

Note that construction and finishing of store interior will begin after approval of design package and finishes after landlord work is almost completed in reference to walls and ceiling.

Some fixtures will be readily available and not require 8 weeks.

In order to shorten the process, approvals must happen quickly and _____ and GMG must have open lines of communication. It is very possible to shorten the process 3-4 weeks.

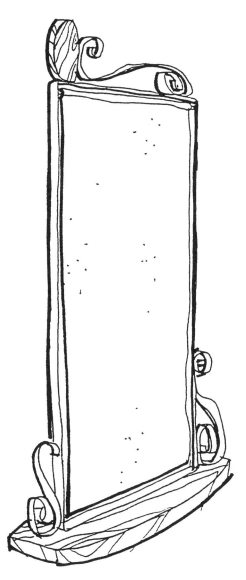

WORKING WITH RESOURCES

Once the design and materials have started to be defined for the project, the resourcing begins. It is important to consider options similar to the first choice if possible as long as they support the overall design concept. It may very well save many dollars.

Working with the designer, approach the suggested resources and request costs. If the client has recommendations based on past experiences or word-of-mouth suggestions, they should be considered. Always discuss in as great of detail necessary all submitted costs if there is some confusion, lack of understanding or higher-than-anticipated costs. Any good resource should be willing to define and answer your questions. At the same time, you may receive low bids that require explanation to get a comfort level with the products, services, etc.

When purchasing products, the terms of each company for payment may vary. It is important to work with letters of commitment or purchase orders to avoid possible confusion. Verbal orders and requests can be confusing and get complicated in the long term of the project.

It is very important to fully understand the fabrication and shipping lead times involved with all necessary items being ordered. This will better assist with installation scheduling. Keep in mind that with manufacturing and shipping there are at times outside controls that unexpectedly delay committed dates. This is very common as are shorter lead times than expected. Custom items generally require longer lead times as do those items that are not sitting on shelves ready to ship.

The list on the following page will introduce some lead times for general products used in retail store design after placement of orders.

- Carpet/floorcoverings .... 2-6 weeks
- Lighting .... 2-4 weeks
- Standard display fixtures .... 2-3 weeks
- Custom display fixtures .... 6-10 weeks
- Standard fixture hardware .... 2-3 weeks
- Custom fixture hardware .... 4-6 weeks
- Graphics and signage .... 3-4 weeks
- Exterior signage .... 4-5 weeks

If you have questions regarding the integrity of resources, it is understandable to request photos from previous projects and references that can be contacted. Legitimate resources will never have problems with such requests if they are interested in working with you. At the same time, a store owner or designer should not be insulted if the project request is considered too small for the resource. Respect for mutual honesty is better received than misleading information.

STORE IDENTITY

The name of your store was chosen for a particular reason. Maybe it's a person's name, product, state of mind and so on, or combinations of many things. It is, however, your chief identifier to the world. It is your business. It's YOU!

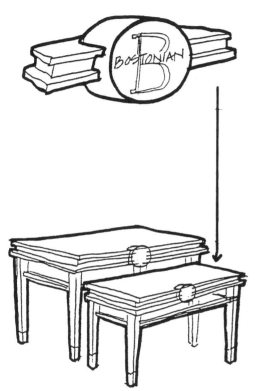

Aside from the actual word or phrase that is your name, it is a symbol with a certain personality. It conveys an image supporting or complementing the store and products for sale. Name, design and logo color should be harmonious with the overall store and shopping experience.

STORE LOGO
Your store identity is not just a name. Your identity can also be a logo, emblem or a mark. It should relate to the store image, name and be a part of everything that conveys or supports the store.

The logo can be a part of the storefront signage, shopping bags, in-store signage and graphics, even the fixturing and displays.

STOREFRONT SIGNAGE
This isn't simply the placement of or use of the store name, but it's also part of the overall store image. Keep in mind the typeface, color, scale and placement. Be imaginative and original. Storefront signage should attract attention while making a statement to passersby and customers.

Remember, never lose focus of the overall store image.

IN-STORE SIGNAGE
Many retailers fail to maintain the complete store image when they introduce in-store signage. Store owners must realize these signs and/or graphics support the entire store environment too.

Many times the in-store signage looks like an afterthought.

Think about the size and color of the sign and copy. Consider its scale in comparison to the actual merchandise. Carefully consider placement and means of attaching signs on fixtures or displays.

SIGN HOLDERS
Does your store require a new sign holder or framing package to strengthen the signage statement? If so, consider the many materials available to you. If necessary, you can design a custom package to support your image. However, many resources carry standard sizes in plastic, metal and wood. For instance, you may decide to use clear acrylic designs that can be frameless pockets providing a front and back cover. When sign holders are used on the sales floor both sides are exposed. Remember, as part of the graphic and signage message, many eyes see the sign holders.

PROMOTIONAL
Retailers just can't get away from the need to promote sales, clearances or specials. However, keep in mind that it should be different than everyday signage. Many retailers use red, orange and yellow to convey the sale message. You might want to use another bright color. Why be like everyone else?

GRAPHICS
This category does not include typical printed message signs. Effective graphics, such as photography or artwork, support merchandise, lifestyle and store image. Introducing graphics to a store interior makes brand or trend messages stronger. Well-placed graphics also break up long runs of merchandise and offer the eye a visual rest from shopping.

Many graphics are made available from vendors and manufacturers often at no charge when merchandise is purchased. Remember that just because a vendor provides a freebie or a low-cost item, it doesn't mean it automatically supports your overall store image. At times, professionally designed custom graphic packages are the best way to go. This allows your store to have a completely different image from the competition.

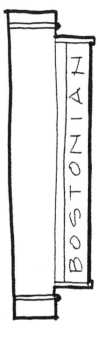

SIDE VIEW
BANNER COLUMN

DEPARTMENTAL IDENTIFICATION

Some retailers prefer to use printed support to merchandise areas for identification. Keep in mind scale, coloration, materials and installation of the sign. Make sure signs complement, and don't overpower, presentations.

CLASSIFICATION SIGNAGE

Depending on the size of your particular store, it's important to identify specific products or complete classifications of merchandise. The same rule of thumb applies here as with departmental identification. Classification signage should typically be smaller than departmental signs, unless it is being used as such.

BRAND IDENTIFICATION

Calling out brand or vendor shops is quite acceptable, especially when properly used in supporting store image. These shops identify important merchandise groups within your store. They can also help separate you from your competition. Remember, vendors offer brand identification on a regular basis in the form of graphics, signage, even displays. Use them with caution, making sure, of course, they support your store image.

VENDOR DISPLAYS

This topic is included since it has a direct correlation to overall image.

Typically these items are mass produced and intended for a limited-time use. They can be important for promotions or sales and new product introductions. However, having said that, often using these displays offers a quick way to compromise a store image. Such displays are generally ideal for gas stations, convenience and discount stores.

Not all vendor displays are of inferior quality. They are usually well thought out and manufactured. Some are better than others. Some are even well-designed and of fixture-grade quality for more permanent use within the store.

P.O.P. GRAPHIC UNIT

MERCHANDISE PRESENTATION

The term "merchandise presentation" is sometimes confused with display or visual merchandising. Merchandise presentation refers to most basic ways of presenting merchandise in an orderly, understandable, easy-to-shop and find-the-product format. It's folded merchandise on shelves or tables or hanging merchandise on freestanding floor fixtures or wall face-outs. It's items stacked on shelves or under a table for support inventory.

Planogram is a word best used. A planogram allows for the arrangement of merchandise on a given fixture to support sales through proper placement by style, price point or sell-through and inventory.

Typically, establishing a planogram is the first step of the process that will end with visual merchandising. However, this is the most important step with regard to store/merchandise housekeeping and maintenance on a daily basis. It's typically the part of a store that remains constant longer than the display above the product.

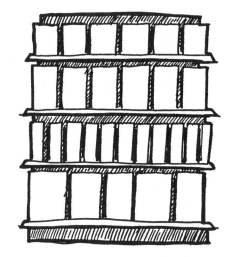

It doesn't mean that the plan is not subject to change, because it is. It simply means that it is not the part of a presentation or display area that is most exciting. The attention is not necessarily supposed to be given to the presentation of the merchandise. The main purpose is to support and enhance the display in a neat, organized manner.

It is not to say that basic merchandise presentation areas must be and always are boring. There are ways, and more importantly times, when breaking the rhythm of flow of merchandise is very important.

Shown on the following pages are examples of quick design sketches that were part of a basic presentation for a particular client. They are intended to show different approaches to adding interest to perimeter walls.

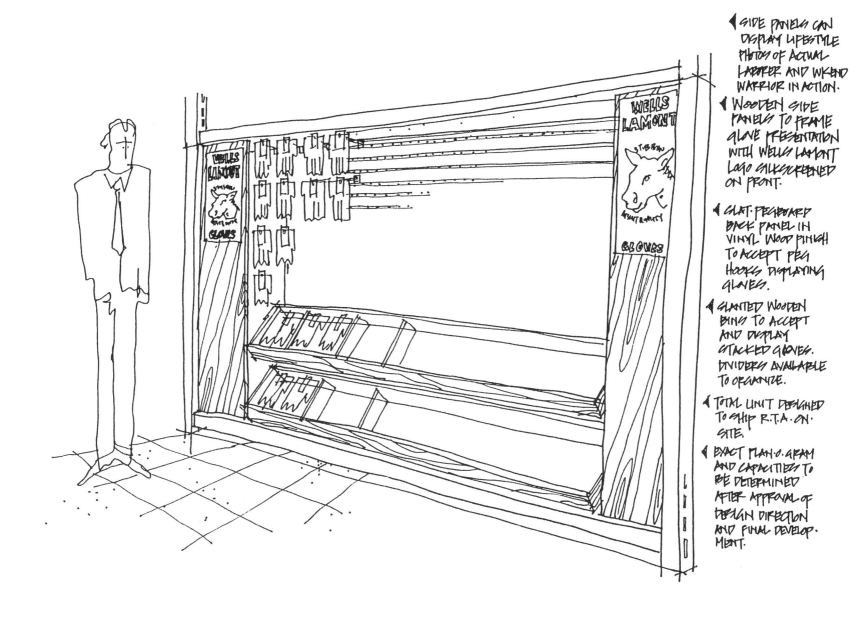

SIDE PANELS CAN DISPLAY LIFESTYLE PHOTOS OF ACTUAL LABORER AND WKEND WARRIOR IN ACTION.

WOODEN SIDE PANELS TO FRAME GLOVE PRESENTATION WITH WELLS LAMONT LOGO SILKSCREENED ON FRONT.

SLAT PEGBOARD BACK PANEL IN VINYL WOOD FINISH TO ACCEPT PEG HOOKS DISPLAYING GLOVES.

SLANTED WOODEN BINS TO ACCEPT AND DISPLAY STACKED GLOVES. DIVIDERS AVAILABLE TO ORGANIZE.

TOTAL UNIT DESIGNED TO SHIP R.T.A. ON SITE.

EXACT PLAN-O-GRAM AND CAPACITIES TO BE DETERMINED AFTER APPROVAL OF DESIGN DIRECTION AND FINAL DEVELOPMENT.

45

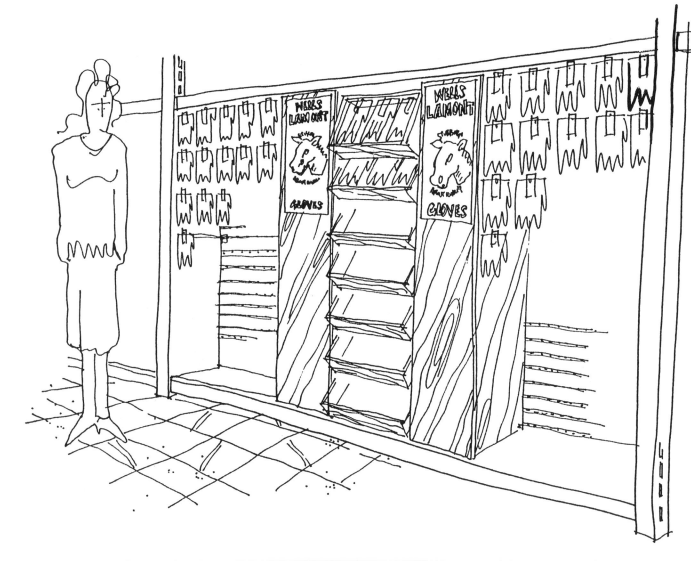

◄ SOLID CENTER WOOD PANELS WITH LOGO AT TOP EACH SIDE OF SLANTED BINS.

◄ SIDE DISPLAY AREAS WITH SLATPEG BACK PANEL TO ACCEPT PEG HOOKS.

◄ DESIGNED AS R.T.A. UNIT ASSEMBLED ON SITE.

◄ EXACT PLAN-O-GRAM AND CAPACITIES TO BE DETERMINED AFTER APPROVAL OF DESIGN DIRECTION AND FINAL DVLPMT.

◄ FRONT TOPPER
VALANCE ABOVE
PEGGED GLOVE
DISPLAYS.
OPTIONAL FLUORESCENT
STRIP LIGHT AVAILABLE

◄ PEGGED MDSE. ON
SLAT PEG.

◄ CENTER AREA WITH
LARGE LOGO PANEL,
WOODEN SHELVES
AND SIDE PANELS.
OPTIONAL LIGHT BOX
INTERNALLY
ILLUMINATED FOR
LOGO PANEL.

◄ DESIGNED AS R.T.A.
ON SITE.

◄ EXACT PLAN·O·GRAM
AND CAPACITIES TO
BE DETERMINED AFTER
APPROVAL OF DESIGN
DIRECTION AND FINAL
DEVELOPMENT.

◄ ADDITIONAL WOOD
VERTICAL DIVIDERS
CAN BE ADDED TO
DEFINE CATEGORIES

When merchandising, make sure that all surfaces are covered as much as possible, increasing merchandise intensity. Wall areas should be tight to avoid exposed wall surfaces and sending the message that inventory is low. Keep in mind that certain stores will require different approaches and that a high end salon may purposely expose wall areas to appear more exclusive. There are always exceptions to merchandising guidelines. Find the one that works best for you and follow it until, possibly, it needs to be updated and/or changed.

There are many resources that provide free or at a minimal charge copies of merchandise guidelines based on their specific product offerings. They plan for inventory control and even increased sales. Ask your sales representative if his/her company has anything available to review for application in your store.

VISUAL MERCHANDISING

This is often referred to as display or trimming. Whatever the term, it is the excitement that complements the basic merchandise presentation on a fixture or wall area. Visual merchandising however, must complement the total store image. It cannot stand alone and always make the store. It's only a part of the total picture.

The manner in which you enhance merchandise within your store can determine and suggest to the customer single or multiple sales. When a variety of items are used together, they can offer the customer a means of understanding how each individual item works as well as how they enhance or support the others.

For example, if you were selling staple guns, you could augment the merchandising message by adding staples in various sizes, an apron or carrying case and possibly a mannequin to wear the apron with a work shirt, hat and gloves.

Another example would be cookware. By adding cookbooks, aprons, utensils and even food, you enhance a presentation that may be otherwise very simple and boring. To further enhance, you could add a mannequin for the human factor, wearing the apron and a hat or T-shirt. It may even be appropriate to add a piece of furniture, tablecloths, napkins and place settings.

Extending a display to incorporate related goods is known as cross-merchandising. It's a very powerful selling tool. Keep in mind however that a certain level of creativity is required to ensure a tasteful presentation. Also, when arranging the merchandising, make sure the message you send is clear. Keep the presentation focused.

Before setting up a display of this kind, plan accordingly. Walk through your store and make notes on what will work together. Then do a few quick sketches to understand the composition of the presentation. Is it a color, fashion or lifestyle statement you wish to make?

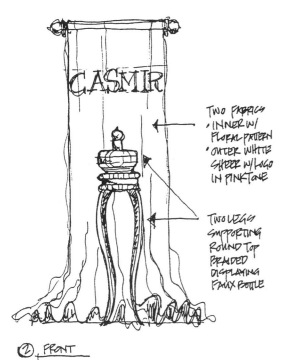

CASMIR

TWO FABRICS
• INNER W/ FLORAL PATTERN
• OUTER WHITE SHEER W/LOGO IN PINK TONE

TWO LEGS SUPPORTING ROUND TOP BRAIDED DISPLAYING FAUX BOTTLE

① FRONT

There are eight basic steps that can be applied to creating a successful display or focal point in your store.

1. EVALUATE THE POTENTIAL DISPLAY AREAS WITHIN YOUR STORE OR DEPARTMENT AND ALLOCATE THE EXACT SPACE.

There are many different available locations to support visual merchandising programs. Stand in front of the store or area and make notes about what you see and where. Use the list below as a starting point in your research:

• Storefront Windows. There are two different types of windows, closed backs and open backs. The exception may be partially open and closed. While windows are important in most situations, open backs should never be filled completely, nor should the display block view into the store. If there are backs to the windows, plan to use the backs inside the store for merchandising. Lighting is important in windows since they are in the storefront. Illumination at night is important even after store hours. Suspended metal or plastic grid panels on the ceiling will allow for hanging-sign flexibility as required.

• Tops of freestanding floor fixtures. Displays should complement the merchandise below and typically be approximately 24"-36" in height if the use of a mannequin alternative is required. Floor fixtures may be metal racks, wood or metal gondolas, tables, pedestals, and furniture.

• Endcaps of fixture runs. This would apply in stores that require longer runs of fixtures allowing for fewer individual opportunities.

• Walls. Application may start at the floor, only be a portion of the upper area, 36"-84", or be above the typical merchandise height of 84".

• Cash wrap counter or service area. Corners can be used to tell simple and short stories but should not be large and cluttering. This area will not work in all stores and should

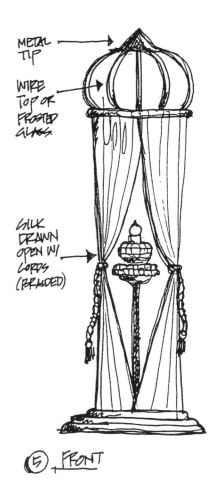

METAL TIP

WIRE TOP OR FROSTED GLASS

SILK DRAWN OPEN W/ CORDS (BRAIDED)

⑤ FRONT

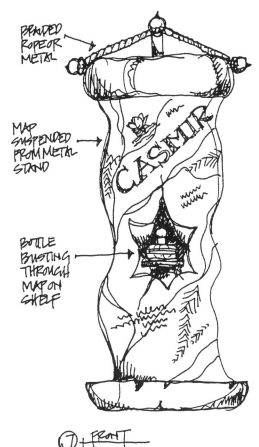

BRAIDED ROPE OR METAL

MAP SUSPENDED FROM METAL STAND

BOTTLE BUSTING THROUGH MAP ON SHELF

CASMIR

7 + FRONT

actually be part of the initial major plan when desired. Keep in mind that the wall area behind the cash wrap is also a wonderful opportunity because most customers typically enter that area at one time or another.

2. DETERMINE THE OVERALL MESSAGE YOU WISH TO SEND THE CUSTOMER AND THE MAIN FOCUS OF THE DISPLAY AREA. IS IT A MAJOR OR MINOR FOCAL DISPLAY?

Is it a seasonal thematic message, sale or price issue, or a new product introduction? The size of the overall display area will dictate importance and definitely the impact. However, smaller, minor displays require less time to set-up and maintain.

3. EVALUATE THE MERCHANDISE TO BE DISPLAYED, COMPLEMENTARY ITEMS, AND AMOUNT OF MERCHANDISE TO SUPPORT THE PRESENTATION.

Display focals should always highlight certain merchandise selections or types based on changes, trends, seasonal demands or even great pricing promotions. When mixing complementary merchandise groups, this is referred to as cross-merchandising.

4. ESTABLISH THE REQUIRED PROPS, FIXTURES AND TOOLS REQUIRED TO CONSTRUCT AND ADD INTEREST.

Review the merchandise listing, then determine best complements of display props and even fixtures. Use a separate checklist and secure all items prior to starting the project.

5. DETERMINE IF SIGNAGE IS AN INTEGRAL PART OF THE OVERALL VISUAL MESSAGE.

Signage should always compliment and never overpower the merchandise unless the message is purely a focal direction. This is one area in which exceptions will occur. Large graphics serve as great backdrops. Large graphics can at times stand alone without merchandise support if the photographic image is merchandise itself. Pricepoint signs should not be considered as an integral part of a display area and have promotional application only.

6. DETERMINE EXACTLY HOW MUCH TIME IS NECESSARY TO START AND COMPLETE THE VISUAL AREA. IS IT A MAJOR OR MINOR FOCAL?

Proper planning can alleviate confusion and delayed completion.

7. CREATE AND EVALUATE THE FOCAL, FINE TUNE AS NECESSARY. LOOK AT THE FOCAL FROM MANY DIFFERENT ANGLES. MAKE SURE THAT THE LIGHTING IS CORRECTLY ADJUSTED ON THE MAIN PART OF THE AREA.

Visual display focal areas are commonly viewed in the round and not necessarily just from the front. Balance the visual impact from all areas.

Too often the lighting is not included but should never be forgotten. Remember that where the light is focused, the eye will typically be drawn to that spot.

8. MAINTENANCE OF THE FOCAL.

Merchandise is often touched, moved, or removed completely for purchase. Make sure that product inventory is always adequate, neat and orderly. Constant review throughout store hours is required.

The best approach is to establish and follow a regularly planned display program for the store. By use of a calendar, strategically plan the store for the next year. Make sure that there is always something of interest for the customer to come back and see in the store. If the store is always exciting, fun and fresh, the customer will continue to return regularly.

Using a calendar will help you to plan adequate time to obtain required materials. It will also enable store management to better understand how much money should be set aside for a regular program.

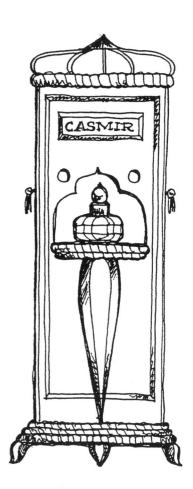

MAY

SUNDAY	MONDAY	TUESDAY	WEDNESDAY	THURSDAY	FRIDAY	SATURDAY
	Labor Day (Mexico) May Day **1**	**2**	**3**	National Day of Prayer **4**	Cinco de mayo (Mexico) **5**	Nurses' Day **6**
7	**8**	**9**	**10**	**11**	**12**	Visual Marketing & Store Design Show, ICFF, and National Sationery Show in New York City 13-16 **13**
Mother's Day **14**	**15**	**16**	**17**	**18**	**19**	Armed Forces Day **20**
Surtex Show 21-23 **21**	Victoria Day (Canada) **22**	**23**	**24**	**25**	School picnic and carnival **26**	Local pools open **27**
28	Memorial Day (Observed) **29**	Memorial Day **30**	**31**			

Sample month

SUNDAY	MONDAY	TUESDAY	WEDNESDAY	THURSDAY	FRIDAY	SATURDAY

Blank month for reproduction

VISUAL MERCHANDISING TOOLS AND SUPPLIES

In order to complete the installation of the display and focal areas, you will require certain tools and hardware.

At the same time, you will need to have a tote bag or tool/storage box to hold everything. It's important to always know where the tools are when they are needed to avoid wasted time. Also, remember to replace any item that is broken or lost.

Use this checklist to build your display tool kit:

_____ Glass Cleaner	_____ Cotton Gloves	_____ Push Pins
_____ X-acto® Knife	_____ Hammer	_____ Aspirin
_____ Utility Knife	_____ Rubber Mallet	_____ Band-Aids
_____ Knife Blades	_____ Screwdrivers	_____ Dust Cloths
_____ Fishing Line	_____ Cordless Drill	_____ Square
_____ Pencils/Sharpener	_____ Tape Measure	_____ Level
_____ Thumb Tacks	_____ Scale	_____ Wire
_____ Spray Adhesive	_____ Iron	_____ Plastic Ties
_____ Rubber Bands	_____ Ironing Board	_____ String
_____ Straight Pins	_____ Steamer	_____ Safety Pins
_____ Hot Glue Gun	_____ Square	_____ Glue Sticks
_____ Assorted Nails	_____ Super Glue	_____ Assorted Screws
_____ Wood Glue	_____ Masking Tape	_____ Staple Gun
_____ Celophane Tape	_____ Staples	_____ Assorted Markers
_____ Scissors	_____ Double Sided Tape	_____ Velcro Strips/Buttons

You will also require a ladder, step stool, wood, paint, brushes, etc., from time to time on some projects.

Make your own list, start acquiring the tools and securing an area within the store for storage of everything when not in use.

VISUAL MERCHANDISING PROPS AND DISPLAYS

Cost doesn't have to be a major factor in achieving successful focal displays in your windows, walls or on the sales floor. Yes, some support props and displays will obviously tend to cost more than others. But if properly planned and utilized, these investments can be very inexpensive and worthwhile in the long run.

For example, if you purchased an armoire to display merchandise and planned to use it for at least a couple of years in various locations throughout your store, its cost could be amortized over several years. The armoire can be used as a fixture on the sales floor or made into a prop for window displays. It can display linens, boxed merchandise, candles or any gift item. If the shelves are adjustable, then the armoire can accept many different types of merchandise. You might want to install lights inside at the top and perhaps even under the shelves.

You may even find that armoire, or something similar, at a garage sale or auction. It may very well be that you have items in your home that could be used for specific periods of time and then rotated out and replaced by something else.

Props and displays could even be throw-aways as in the case of wooden crates, covered boxes, foamboard cut-outs, corrugated elements and the like.

Props can be seasonal or used throughout the year. Sometimes it's only a matter of a new coat of paint to update or change an item. Tablecloths can be used to cover items completely or even be partially exposed.

Items that are sold in your store can also be used as support props. For example, if you sell chairs and folded towels, they could be used together.

If possible, display props can be ticketed and sold upon request. This enables the store to be able to purchase new replacement items adding new interest to the overall store.

– WOODEN PAINTED
SOCKS AND SHOES
3A

MERCHANDISING BY COLOR

Vertical and horizontal presentation underlie color merchandising, Vertical allows greater exposure to merchandise than the horizontal approach and thereby requires a separate approach.

It also organizes the color palette, which increases visual impact and sales. The typical starting point is the left side on the wall. All colors should be light to dark starting with warm colors and ending with cool ones.

If the need exists to tell a color story on one single hardware faceout, utilize the light to dark technique again, front to back.

When telling color stories on freestanding floor fixtures such as a four way rack, place light colors on a faceout directly facing the aisle. Going clockwise, darks getting darker.

If ever in doubt, reference a color wheel. Listed below is a version of that approach as well as other characteristics of color:

PRIMARY COLORS - Red, yellow, and blue
SECONDARY COLORS - Orange, green and purple, which are formed by mixing the primary colors.
TERTIARY COLORS - Colors created by mixing the primary and secondary colors, such as yellow-green, blue-green, blue-violet, red-violet, red-orange, and yellow-orange.

Colors are also referenced in relation to temperatures and the feelings they evoke:

WARM COLORS - Red, yellow and orange
COOL COLORS - Blue, green and purple

Lastly, colors are seen as associated with human characteristics:

Yellow -   Caution, cowardice, treachery, madness
Red -   Passion, love
Orange -   Knowledge, warmth, energy, force
Violet -   Royalty, depression
Blue -   Fidelity, sobriety, fear
Green -   Wealth, outdoors, luck, nature
Brown -   Maturity, humility
White -   Purity, truth
Black -   Death, depression, sorrow

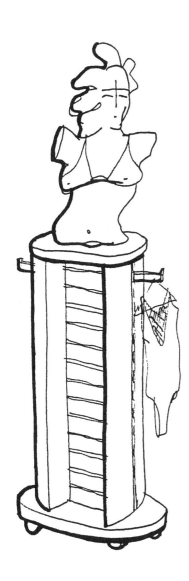

BASIC PRINCIPLES OF DESIGN AND VISUAL DISPLAY CREATION

1. SHAPE OR PATTERNS
The shape is dictated somewhat by the area in which the display will be placed.

Single unit -   single prop or mannequin form dressed
Pyramid -   use of same/similar products forming this shape through stacking;
                  props can be used to support the basic pyramid
Step -   gradual increases of product height with or without support props
Fan -   objects are arranged radiating from a central object or point
Line -   marking of points along or to form a straight or curved mark
Grid -   square of cube approach with various design approaches to height

2. BALANCE
Specifically this relates to positioning of items with reference to amount of space between and weight of object locations.

Symmetrical - when two sides are equal in visual weight and appearance
Asymmetrical- one side has greater presence or weight attracting the eye more than the other side, off center

3. PROPORTION
The relative sizes of items or product in comparison to the space around them.

4. DOMINANCE
The use of one single item larger than others or accented by light so that it stands out separate from them.

5. RHYTHM
Movement of the eye once it has come into contact with the specific display area.

6. REPETITION

Reinforcing and strengthening the impression through replication of an object or shape.

7. MOVEMENT

The actual use of motors or other mechanical means.

8. COLOR

Lighter and brighter colors tend to attract the eye first.

Colors are a very personal part of our lives. However, when designing a store or focal point, keep in mind that it is for the customer or in support of the overall store image.

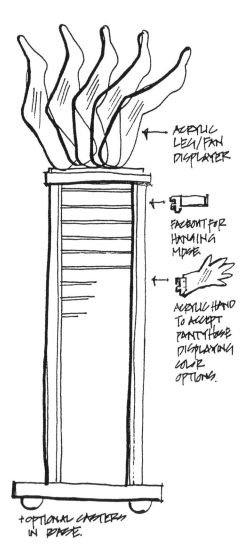

ACRYLIC LEG/FAN DISPLAYER

FACEOUT FOR HANGING MDSE.

ACRYLIC HAND TO ACCEPT PANTYHOSE DISPLAYING COLOR OPTIONS.

+OPTIONAL CASTERS IN BASE.

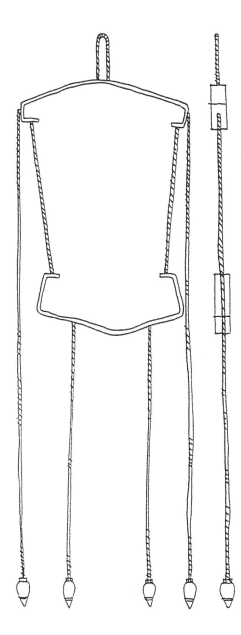

MANNEQUINS AND ALTERNATIVES

The use of mannequins in retail store design has typically been directly related to visual excitement. However, more important is the introduction of the human form in the overall design. It is a natural to have these tools in apparel areas, but don't forget non-apparel areas to introduce personality and dimension.

Mannequins are typically expensive and unless used on a regular basis by educated individuals in the visual merchandising industry, are difficult or time consuming to change and dress. However, the overall effect is a wonderful complement. There are companies that do sell mostly used and refurbished mannequins. One factor that offers personality is the mannequin head. Yet at the same time, the head and the mannequin's positions are the first elements to limit use over time and with application. For example, if you use a very traditional head design, it may not work in a younger, more contemporary application. A sitting mannequin cannot be used for height and a standing mannequin will never sit.

One recommendation if actual mannequins are desired is to consider headless versions with decorative neck blocks. Removable head options are also popular because they allow for better flexibility.

The most basic form of a mannequin alternative is a simple bent or straight metal rod to serve as shoulders and a vertical rod for height. If desired, the vertical rod can be flexible allowing for change in height as required. While this form is inexpensive, it doesn't allow for as much dimension as shoulders provide.

The happy medium is to have dimensional shoulders made of plastic, cast resin or wood on top of the metal upright. Note that alternatives may be full or half height. To increase the dimension, a chest plate can be added. Also note, that with only shoulders, the mannequin alternative is a uni-sex design with greatest flexibility throughout the store.

Forms are typically referred to as parts of the human anatomy that don't rely on upright support members and simply sit on top of a fixture or hook onto a wall system with special brackets. Forms most commonly used are upper torsos without arms, waist and partial thighs, full legs, arms, hands, feet and heads.

When dressing mannequins and alternatives, there are certain points to keep in mind:

1. LAYERING

Layering can also be recognized as being a silent salesman showing the customer a complete ensemble or wardrobe that works together. When the customer doesn't have a lot of time to spend looking and coordinating this is a very important time saving and profitable cross-merchandising approach.

An example of layering is a t-shirt under a shirt under a jacket. To give it the extra touch, neck wear, jewelry or other accessories may be added.

2. BOTTOM OF CLOTHING

Some items will naturally taper at the ends however, typically, the clothing will simply hang if not attended to in another way. One approach is to gather the bottom with a belt, scarf or tie. Another would be to fold like pleats and pin together. Make sure to pull tight the clothing being pinned, eliminating unnecessary wrinkles.

3. STUFFING THE CLOTHING

If absolutely necessary, foam inserts or crinkled tissue paper can be inserted to add dimension and form to otherwise flat-hanging merchandise. Be sure to contain the stuffing inside by tapering the garment at the bottom.

4. STEAMING AND IRONING

All wrinkles should be removed and pleats pressed when items are used on display.

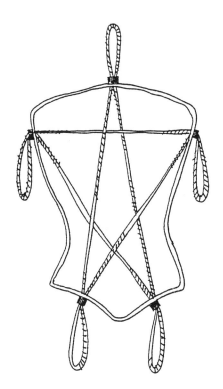

5. INCLUDING PANTS AND BOTTOMS

If the mannequin alternative is full height it may have a pant bar to accept pants. If not, simply pin the pants to the top portion. side facing is very commonly used since it presents the bottom in a neat and orderly manner. Pin the bottom of the legs and weight to pull taut.

There are times with certain mannequin forms that actual pant bars are a part of the display allowing folded pants to hang in front of the tops. However, if not, it is possible to creatively fold and hang pants over shoulders as a complement.

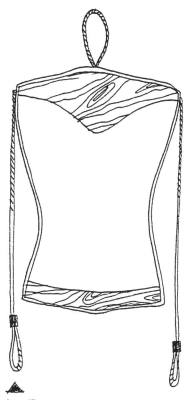

BENT FLAT WIRE TORSO FRAME, WOODEN SHOULDER AND WAIST INSERTS WITH CABLE HANGER AND ARM EXTENSIONS.

INTERIOR FOCAL POINTS

BE CREATIVE
BE IMAGINATIVE
ADD EXCITEMENT
MAKE A STATEMENT
BE DRAMATIC
DON'T HOLD BACK
THINK BIG
CREATE FUN
SHOW PERSONALITY
EDUCATE THE CUSTOMER
TELL A STORY
ROMANCE THE PRODUCT
TAKE RISKS
CHANGE IS GOOD

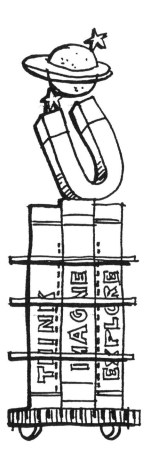

No matter what buzz words or catchy phrases are in, the message is always the same, whether it's a simplistic approach or highly detailed. It doesn't make any difference if it's for hard or soft goods.

You have a very limited amount of time to catch the attention of the passerby and turn her into a customer. Statistics vary from 7 to 10 seconds for the target time to catch the eye of the customer to your store. You owe it to yourself to give thought to what they will be looking at that represents your store's image during those few seconds.

The display just inside the store is the most important in many cases. It's center stage, and may even be elevated to draw greater attention to itself. It could be a display vehicle like a table or piece of furniture. Mannequins could be included wearing merchandise even if yours isn't primarily an apparel store. This added dimension can be that special touch required. It is also important to show how certain items can be used. You may even indicate new ways to use old items.

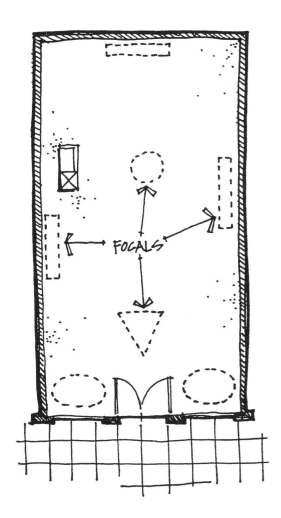

The customer will be able to view and experience particular focal points due to planned sightlines within your store as part of the design. It is important to make sure that these areas have impact and are strategically located. It's important to have these areas balanced throughout the sales floor.

When customers enter your store, they should easily identify specific areas by the use and placement of focal points. For example, the left wall is the kitchen area, back wall dedicated to casual dining and the right wall to display accessories for the remainder of the home. Each area has at least one main wall focal that support minor focal points on the sales floor. If necessary or desired, the areas can contain signage denoting each area. However, by the use of large lifestyle photo-graphics the areas can make the same statement without being as direct.

The focal areas need to be carefully thought out and planned since they will be the main image statements. These areas should be maintained daily and kept fresh. Rotation of product in the interior focal areas is as important as the storefront windows. As seasons change or new merchandise arrives, the focuses should reflect the items or promote the incentive to purchase seasonal items. Plan changes on a regular basis with the use of a calendar. It is not too often to change all or partial portions of the displays weekly.

Another tip is to simply rotate or move focal displays from one location to another within the respected areas or departments. This also gives the same impact of change and newness. To ensure the impact and add more meaning to focal displays, use cross-merchandising techniques.

Specific planned areas on the walls should be turned into focal areas, visually merchandised to stand out from the rest of the presentation. These areas work in much the same manner as those referenced just inside the storefront. Wall vignettes are also supported by freestanding displays on the floor in front of them.

These great merchandising areas offer opportunity since they can be seen from far above and beyond those on the floor.

One of the best ways to add personality and life to these displays is through cross-merchandising. For example, if your store sells garden utensils, plants, pots, hand tools, tables, chairs and some apparel, this is a complete story. This is much more exciting and attention getting than simple stacks of clay pots with, one plant in the top. It's suggestive selling, and it shows the customer related items that in one focused area.

The stock to support the display should be close for the customer to locate and examine, possibly in various colors and sizes. The use of mannequins or mannequin alternatives is not beyond reason because these elements add dimension as well as the human factor. Mannequins can add great personality and excitement to any situation.

The wall areas need to be balanced and well organized as well. Especially since they are eye-catching. Make sure that the sales associates understand the importance of these areas as selling tools and do not neglect them. Wall focal areas need to be planned and changed regularly just like window displays in the storefront.

You can use paint as a very inexpensive media for wonderful contrast or textures. The entire wall area or simply that which is exposed typically above the general merchandise area can receive the finish, giving a different look periodically throughout the year.

Brand identification letters are often used to call attention to areas as vendor shops or simply to inform the customer that their products are available.

Letters can also be used for departmentalization or specific product recognition. These can be self adhesive backed pre-cut vinyl or dimensional dense foam painted. Colors can be contrasting or tone-on-tone for a more sophisticated approach.

When fixtures are used against the walls as the major focal elements, movement is easily achieved. It allows for growth and/or reduction of certain areas based on seasonal factors.

TRAFFIC FLOW

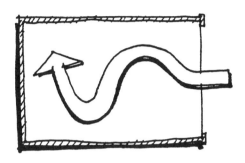

Traffic flow or circulation is vital to the shopping comfort and ease of finding items for the customer. The shopper should not have to think about how to move within the store, but be led through. The actual aisles can be defined by different colors and materials or by merchandise and fixture placement.

Traffic flow can be controlled in the following ways:
• Straight front to back, or side-to-side aisles
• Racetrack, allowing the customer to circle the store
• Meandering paths

Regardless of the approach decided upon, remember that the aisles should be wide enough for the customer to use. Too often aisles are narrow and make it difficult to comfortably walk through a store and even share the aisle with another customer or sales associate.

Also keep in mind that lighting can be used to move the shopper through the store. This is easily done by lighting the aisles and creating focal areas with brighter light to attract and move shoppers through the space.

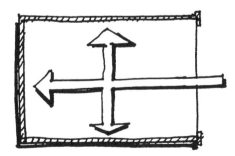

Other reasons for well-defined, wide aisles are for emergency egress and to meet ADA (Americans with Disabilities Act) requirements.

The use of steps and ramps should be thoroughly thought out in support of proper flow. When used, railings are mandatory to avoid accidents and for insurance purposes.

Remember, never make the customer feel trapped or lost in your store. The customer should also never be forced to worry about bumping into merchandise. They should always be able to focus on the merchandise.

Stockroom areas should always have wide aisles clear of merchandise and supplies for easy access.

Be sure to provide adequate area behind and in front of the cashwrap/point-of-sale counter. This is one area that should be open and not crowded.

FIXTURING

When designing your store, make sure that the vehicle that holds your merchandise — the fixturing — is complementary. The fixturing is an extension of the store image. The finishes, materials, textures and scale must also enhance the merchandise.

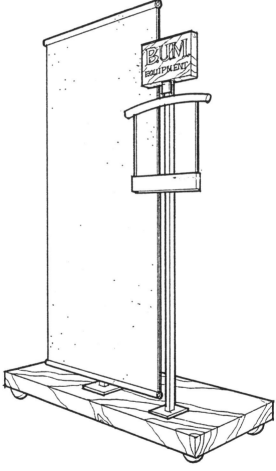

Fixturing can be recognized two ways:
• Simple and functional, or
• Designed to be exposed and have personality

When designing or purchasing ready-made fixtures, think about the types of merchandise it will accept. Think about both short- and long-term usage.

When fixtures are merchandised, they're either merchandise-intense, fixture-intense or a comfortable medium. What are you looking for in your store? What can your store support? What works best with your merchandise — where, when and how?

Fixtures can be focal elements, and can prevent customers from seeing around them. In certain size stores this is necessary to define areas. However, in other stores, fixtures should be lower at the aisle and gradually increase in height as they approach the walls. A combination of these two approaches is ideal when designed and used properly.

Flexibility is typically the best design feature to pursue in fixture design. The main reason for this is to accommodate change in merchandise from season to season. It also adds excitement in the merchandise presentation. The most flexible fixture systems consist of one of the following or a combination:

• Slotted standards (surface mounted or recessed)
• Slatwall panels, standard or reinforced slots
• Slat grid panels
• Pin systems
• Slotted tubing uprights

There are many types of fixtures required to complete a store interior. Some are strictly for merchandise and others are for service-related functions:

• Floor units for hanging merchandise or folded items; these units may also accept stacked or piled merchandise
• Combination/shop units accept both hanging and shelved merchandise groups
• Wall fixtures typically work with hanging and shelved merchandise either flexible or fixed
• Fixed display units can be furniture like that used in residential situations
• Security fixtures such as glass showcases arranged in runs to serve as counters or freestanding walk-around units
• Highlight displays such as single pedestals or small tables to feature a particular item
• Cashwrap/point-of-sale counters along with back counters strictly for storage and work service
• Fitting rooms can be designed for off-site fabrication and then installed on-site
• Some architectural elements may be designed in pieces and assembled on-site to serve as display fixtures

When designing the fixture package for a store, keep in mind the hardware requirements. Note that the hardware needs will change as does the type of merchandise.

Your store may require a vendor or merchandise shop concept to support a specific brand or group of merchandise. In this situation, the fixtures would be different than the rest in order for the shop to be special.

Rotation of fixtures within the space can add freshness to the overall shopping experience. Fixtures can also be rotated for use in display windows. The greater the flexibility of the fixture, the greater the possibility to move around.

If movement is important, add casters to the base.

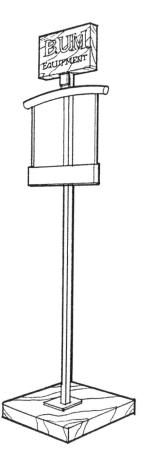

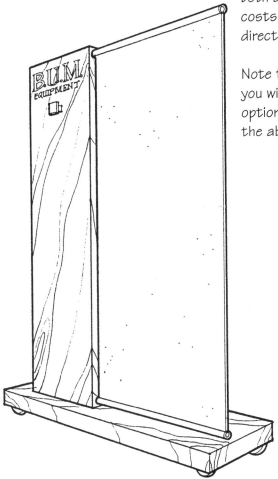

When creating new fixture design concepts, it is important to have an idea of what type of merchandise will be displayed and anticipated costs. This information is important to both a retail store designer and fixture manufacturer. There are ways to value engineering costs out of fixtures, yet still maintain the desired end result. Before deciding on a final direction or unit, entertain many different options.

Note that some fixture manufacturers have in-house design staff capable of providing you with options to approve if you purchase the finished product from them. This is an option if you have a good comfort level with the resource. However, it typically eliminates the ability to secure additional competitive prices for comparison.

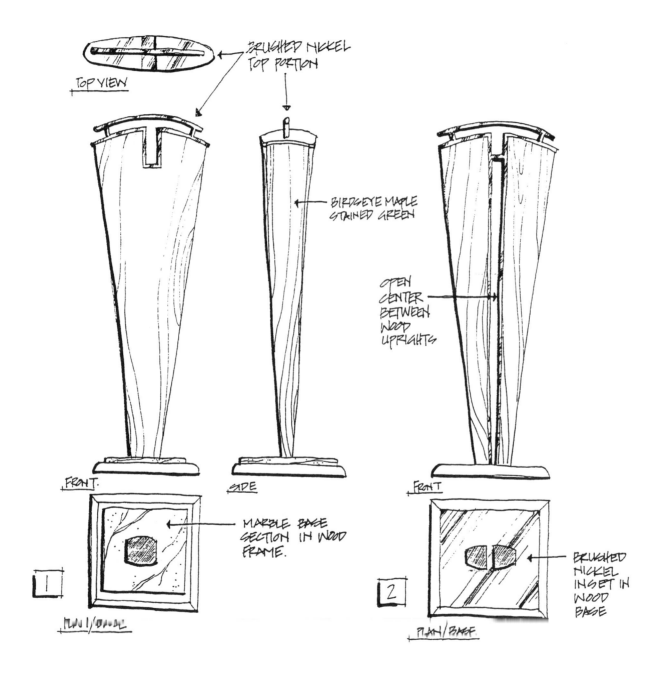

TOP VIEW

BRUSHED NICKEL
TOP PORTION

BIRDSEYE MAPLE
STAINED GREEN

OPEN
CENTER
BETWEEN
WOOD
UPRIGHTS

FRONT

SIDE

FRONT

MARBLE BASE
SECTION IN WOOD
FRAME.

BRUSHED
NICKEL
INSET IN
WOOD
BASE

1

PLAN/BASE

2

PLAN/BASE

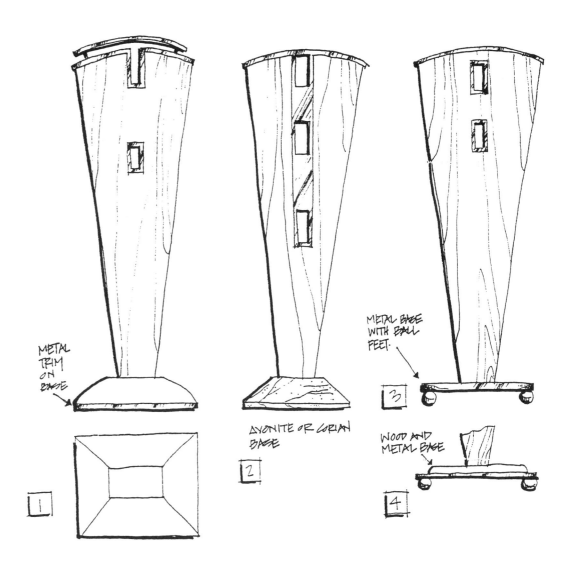

METAL
TRIM
ON
BASE

1

AYONITE OR CORIAN
BASE

2

METAL BASE
WITH BALL
FEET.

3

WOOD AND
METAL BASE

4

LIGHTING

Lighting is an essential and integral part of the visual presentation and store design, yet often ignored. The role of lighting in the development of successful retail environments includes fulfilling the following objectives:

• Provide proper illumination to enhance and dramatize the merchandise
• Establish highlights of the merchandise presentation to distinguish visual organization, excitement and flow through the space
• Create the desired atmosphere and mood throughout the store
• Provide for adequate task lighting for sales associates

Technically speaking, lighting design needs to incorporate four principal objectives:

• Provide correct lumen/light level
• Provide good color rendition of merchandise
• Provide uniformity of light coverage and highlights
• Consider energy conservation

These lighting principles should be applied to retail design using the following categories:

• Ambient lighting
• Perimeter lighting
• Accent lighting
• Task lighting

The proper balance of these types and applications is key to creating an appropriate and successful retail environment. Typically, ambient lighting has the lowest level of intensity. Perimeter walls are brighter to draw the customer to the area. Accent is the brightest to highlight specific floor and wall display areas. Task lighting is used for illuminating work areas.

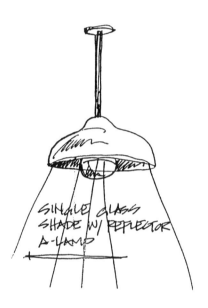

SINGLE GLASS
SHADE W/ REFLECTOR
A-LAMP

Independent small store owners will typically accept from landlords what is referred to as a plain white box. This is so termed since the floor is concrete, walls are unpainted drywall and the ceiling is basic 2' x 4' lay-in acoustical ceiling tiles in a suspended metal T-grid frame system.

With this basic approach, it is no wonder that the actual lighting fixtures are the most basic as well. The most common light fixtures provided are general inexpensive 2' x 4', 3- or 4-lamp fluorescent light fixtures with prismatic lenses. You will find they simply provide general illumination and nothing more.

To start with, the fluorescent fixtures should have electronic ballasts and require T-8 Lamps. These are the most energy efficient units on the market today. However, it is important to note that technology changes rapidly, as does government involvement with energy requirements. The type of lens used is also important. Basic prismatic lens do not allow the most light to be generated out of the fixture and onto the sales floor below. In fact, they tend to capture a percentage of light within the fixture itself. The lens will also discolor over a period of time since the material used for the lens is acrylic. With age, they also will be prone to become brittle and crack easily.

A general rule of thumb is that the more open and exposed the lens, the more light is allowed to travel through and illuminate the area.

The industry standard parabolic louver is injection molded polystyrene plastic, 1/2" x 1/2" x 1/2" cell size, with metalized specular finish. The cell is also available in white. Because this lens is open due to the cells, obviously more light is allowed to travel out of the fixture housing. However, note that the light is forced more downward than wider to the sides with standard acrylic lenses. This will be discussed further under ambient lighting.

To better illuminate the store, additional light sources should be considered. One typical application is to light aisles or main open areas with recessed cans or down lights. These are commonly referred to as cans because the overall shape and design is similar

METAL REFLECTOR
W/ REFLECTOR A-LAMP

to a can. These lights are capable of generating greater light density and intensity in a smaller more focused area. The light source can vary depending on the bulb required. Standard fixtures utilize A lamps, which are common household bulbs, or Par and reflector spots and floods. The most commonly used is the Par spot due to greater light intensity focused as opposed to the flood that will cover a broader area but not as crisp of light.

Due to changes in technology and the search for lower energy consumption, there is a unit that utilizes compact fluorescent bulbs.

When looking for the right recessed down light to meet your needs, you will find many options available in finishes, add-on lenses, louvers, even adjustability of the light source. The two basic types of units to consider are fixed and adjustable. The fixed does not allow for movement in the direction of the light beam. This works well because there is never a need for adjustment. So often when a lamp burns out and is replaced, the person who completed the task did not think to readjust the lamp in the right direction on product or graphics. There are attachments available called wall washer baffles that will direct the light, if required, on an angle. These are typically used along wall areas. It is important to understand that the baffle is moveable and will require adjustment.

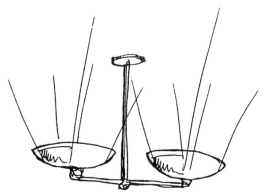

TWO-LAMP UP-LIGHT
W/ GLASS GLOBES

Adjustable lighting is perfect when you know that there will be a need to control and adjust the light beam in a general area. For example, in a large open display area or on walls where the actual focal point moves. Just remember, always adjust correctly when changing lamps. It is often suggested that this be a two person task so that the person on the ladder doesn't have to constantly climb up and down. However, there are tools on the market today that allow you to stand on the floor and remove and install lamps easily. Contact your local light source or fixture display resource for more information on bulb changers.

The third type of light source is track lighting. It is so named because the light source/ fixture is installed on a track or circuit. It can be installed vertically or horizontally on walls and ceilings. Track lighting can be mounted directly on a surface or suspended with conduit or cables. Manufacturers or electricians performing the installation can supply all necessary accessories. Track is available in standard 4' x 8' sections. It is referred to in starter sections and add-ons. When installing there are fixed and adjustable connectors available to meet the design requirements. While track is not always considered a design element, depending on the store and general feeling, it can be a part of the visual excitement. For example, contrasting black track against a white ceiling will stand out. Track suspended below the standard acoustical or drywall ceiling will actually create the illusion of a lower ceiling by invading the open space.

Track installed on angles help to add personality and even create movement. When considering the use of track lighting systems, think about the functional aspects and design of both. Remember that track lighting is easily moved or relocated if desired and required to adapt to future change.

When installing track lighting along wall areas, I prefer the track to be approximately 4' - 5' from the front of the wall fixture or merchandise. For example, if the wall display fixture is 1'-0" deep, the track would be installed at 5' - 6' from the wall. This is based on a typical ceiling height of 10' -12'.

As mentioned in other parts of the book, low voltage lighting is desirable and required, due to increased energy consumption guide lines from the Federal Government. In some cases the store owner will need to make changes to meet state and local requirements. If your state has strict guide lines, you will need to consult with a lighting engineer or designer who is licensed.

With low-voltage lighting, there is some noise produced by the general system, from the lamps themselves and the transformers, especially if dimmer switches are utilized. This noise can be heard depending on the lamp and transformer combination, level of overall background noise, absorbency factor of surrounding surface materials, and lastly the hearing capabilities of persons in the space.

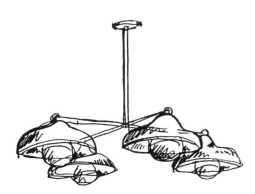

4-GLOBE CHANDELIER

Generally speaking, non-dimmed magnetic transformers cannot be heard by most people. If an area should be as quiet as possible, like an office, gallery, or bookstore, dimmers are not recommended for use. A PAR 36 lamp, for example, generally emits a slight sizzle or buzz sound from the filament when dimmed. Keep in mind that in more open areas the noise will typically not be an issue.

Some fixtures utilize electronic transformers. Specially designed dimmers are available to work with the solid state circuits. However, they will not work with magnetic transformers and are more expensive. The main benefit with electronic transformers is size. They are smaller than magnetic. You will notice that with track lighting, the transformer is enclosed in a housing but still visible. It is possible to install transformers out of sight above the ceiling plain if this is not desired.

For design or decorative purposes, wall-mounted light fixtures, or pendants can be introduced. It is not uncommon to see this application used in support of an overall store image or add extra interest to a specific area within the store.

Other types of lights included in store design from an operational aspect are exit, emergency and night lighting. The landlord is responsible to make sure the space meets the codes, if you do not greatly modify the white box with new wall construction and tall fixtures. Exit lights need to be visible during emergency situations such as a power failure.

At that time, the emergency lighting will automatically turn on and offer general directional lights throughout the store to facilitate movement to safe areas and exits. You will be advised during final lighting inspections by lighting inspectors and fire marshals prior to opening the store if adequate lights have been planned for and installed. While power failures may not happen often, it is extremely important to be properly prepared for the situation if it does occur.

SCHOOL HOUSE
WHITE GLASS
GLOBE SUSPENDED

Tips on how to use accent track lighting and maximize the impact:

When directing track lighting on walls for focal points always aim at angles and not straight onto the area. This will elongate the amount of light on the wall. You can also achieve this by using two fixtures and crossing the beams of light on the intended area. Keep in mind that since you want to accent the focal area, limit lights to the upper wall areas. Allow the overall ambient lighting source to illuminate the rest of the wall areas.

While it is typically thought that flood lamps should be used, the actual light is not as bright and crisp compared to spot lamps. Start with spots, stand back and evaluate the condition. If fixtures are too close to the walls or fixtures you may actually need floods to spread the light beams. However angling will greatly compensate for the light fixture closeness.

The same applies when illuminating glass showcases, especially since the glass has reflective qualities. Lamps should be on an angle from the sides of the cases instead of front or back. When used behind, reflected light will shine in the eyes of the customer. This makes viewing the merchandise very difficult. If angled from the front, the light will be in the eyes of the sales associate.

Showcases should have halogen light sources inside. There are some designs that utilize mini-spots. However, a light source along the entire front will provide even and more adequate lighting and fewer shadows. I do not recommend using light sources in the backs of the cases. This tends to darken the front of the merchandise and can even glare in the eyes of the customer in front of the showcase.

If necessary to provide proper lighting in jewelry departments with showcases, add small task lighting on top of the cases that can be directed onto merchandise. This will allow the sales associates to illuminate the trays and hands of the customer when trying on the jewelry.

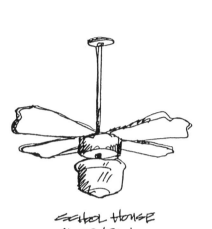

SCHOOL HOUSE
GLOBE / PAN

AMBIENT LIGHTING

The goal in ambient lighting design is to develop a general light level consistent with the merchandise or service. It also allows the customer to distinguish the features, colors and other properties of the merchandise being presented. This may be referred to as general illumination.

Lighting sources that may be considered for this function include:
• Recessed fluorescent or incandescent downlight
• Fluorescent, incandescent or neon cove lighting
• Recessed metal-halide light fixtures, either fixed or adjustable in spot or flood beams
• Surface-mounted track lighting or chandeliers, pendant mounted, even suspended track
• Certain lenses can be introduced to either control the direction or quantity of light

Certain installation configurations are to be considered when laying out a reflected ceiling plan. The options are random or linear. A combination of the two is another possibility.

PERIMETER LIGHTING

Perimeter lighting refers to the illumination of wall areas and merchandise presentation. This lighting is basically general illumination. The main purpose is to light the walls, creating different effects depending on the actual light source used. Some highs and lows can be designed to add excitement. This is easily achieved by mixing different light sources.

Some of the main light fixture sources are as listed:
• Valance or cornice lighting, at top of merchandise or ceiling mounted
• Surface mounted track lighting, either low-voltage or halogen
• Recessed fluorescent or halogen down lights, fixed or adjustable
• Pendant or suspended light sources, possibly custom designed

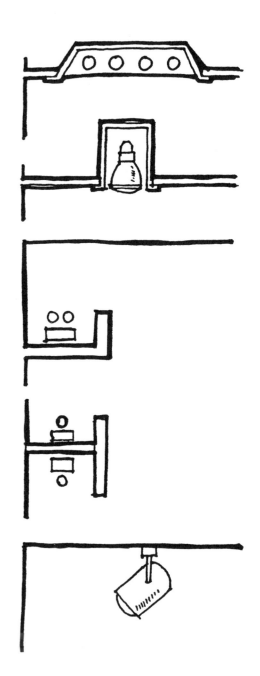

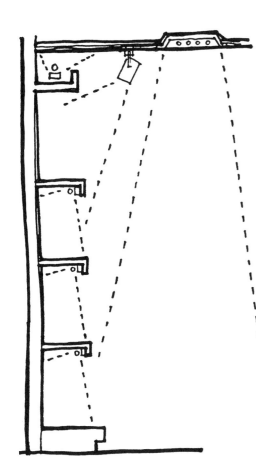

ACCENT LIGHTING

This light source is typically the most dramatic. It provides focus, orientation, and visual impact supporting merchandise presentation and visual merchandising. Sometimes referred to as hot spots (in a positive sense) accent lighting allows specific areas on the walls and sales floor to stand out from the rest of the general illumination. When used properly, it can control traffic flow through a space.

At times, the accent light sources are more detailed and attractive. The fixtures complement the architecture, store image and more importantly, enhance the merchandise statement.

Consider the following fixtures:
• Surface mounted or suspended low-voltage
• Halogen par light fixtures
• Recessed adjustable low-voltage or halogen
• Custom designed light fixtures

TASK LIGHTING

This light source is typically required for detail work at cashwrap/point-of-sale counters, demonstration areas, display counters and the like.

In addition to these areas referenced, it is also important at times to incorporate lighting into the actual display fixtures. Some general applications are under shelves, inside display cases, and inside wall units such as armoires and bookcases.

Make sure that non-sell areas, such as stock rooms and hallways, are brightly illuminated. These work areas are vital to the support of the sales floor and poor light levels will only slow down the process when looking for and retrieving merchandise for the customer.

Maintenance is also a very important facet of the lighting program. If you are taking over an existing store, all of the lamps may not be as efficient, or there may be a wrong combination or mixture of lamps. Quite often, a bulb burns out and it is simply replaced with the first available bulb found. Be sure to always have extra lamps around that are consistent with your original lighting package.

At the same time, the existing light fixtures should be properly cleaned to ensure the greatest reflective quality available. When working with an electrician, you may want your ballasts checked.

If the overall store budget is very tight, the store may open with general illumination light sources with all accent or additional general illumination fixtures added at a later date. This is especially true if at first the visual focal points throughout the store are not defined. However, proper planning should allow for identification of these potential areas prior to opening.

If you have questions, contact a retail store designer, lighting engineer or even a lighting sales representative in regards to your overall lighting needs.

ARCHITECTURAL ELEMENTS AND CEILINGS

As referenced earlier in this book, the typical store starts as a plain white box. With new construction, this is the extent that the landlord is willing to budget for. If the store is existing, it may possess some architectural or ceiling details. Keep in mind that just because details may exist, you don't have to use them "as is." They may not be appropriate for the new store design concept. Plus, trying to work with some existing elements may conflict with the overall image or desired merchandise areas. Therefore, removal or demolition of some or all of the existing unwanted elements must take place. In order to properly plan the project, demolition plans should be drawn in order for the contractor to understand his total scope of work and provide pricing on this part of the project.

When considering permanent architectural elements, remember that if they utilize floor space, they may restrict flexibility in the future, thereby requiring demolition to remove new wall preparations, ceiling work and flooring patches. So, when you plan demising walls between sales and stock room areas, and wall buildouts, plan for long term use of short term increased remodel dollars.

Another way to add or consider architectural treatments, is to not interrupt the floor and lower walls, but use bulkheads and ceiling drops. These occur either directly with the ceiling area alone or on upper wall areas still incorporating the ceiling.

Bulkheads in the ceilings should have a minimum height increase of 1' before starting the next level of ceiling tiles or drywall. This design approach will make the store feel more open in the particular area, whether in the middle of the store, front entrance area or in the rear. Some raised ceiling treatments can be considered along walls also. When utilizing bulkheads, the opportunity does exist to consider additional lighting sources for effect or indirect illumination. Raised ceiling areas can be painted a different color for accent and interest. For example, the raised portion of ceiling could be painted sky blue and possibly receive faux clouds as well.

One approach to take with architectural fixture built-ins is to actually prefabricate in a shop and simply install on-site. If the tops of the units are finished with architectural moldings to the ceiling, they appear to have permanence. This type of fixture approach allows for flexibility and movement at a later date as required. It is typically less expensive to have fixtures built in a shop environment than the actual store, job site. You may even contract with the fixture shop for installation of the fixtures rather than the general contractor. Keep in mind that the general contractor will simply hire the installer and then add his 10 - 20% mark-up. When contracting separately, it may require a slightly greater time commitment on the part of the store owner or store designer to properly coordinate installation.

Another item that can add increased excitement and is not widely used is a platform. Platforms elevate certain merchandise offerings and can serve as a single department, setting it apart from the others.

One of the main negatives against the use of platforms is the added cost involved. The contractor or carpenter must build a structurally sound area above the existing concrete slab floor. In addition, handrails and a ramp must be installed. The railing is for safety purposes around the perimeter. The ramp is to allow direct access for individuals in wheelchairs or with other disabilities.

The ADA, Americans With Disabilities Act, is strongly enforced in most areas and has specific requirements that apply to platforms, ramps and steps. The store designer and/or store owner needs to check with local codes that have jurisdiction over national codes for their area.

When platforms are used, the ceiling height(s) in that area requires attention. Make sure that a minimum of 8 - 9' is maintained.

In some situations a second floor or lower level may exist in a store that the client desires to turn into retail sales floor space. In cases like this the designer will need to take into consideration access, by means of a staircase or elevator. The latter is obviously the more expensive approach. Stairwells can be very exciting locations within store environments. The walls should not be merchandised for safety reasons but can receive paint/wallcoverings, lighting and even graphics and/or visual focal points. The need is to attract customers and direct them to the other level.

During some of my consultations with clients, the recommendations are to either cut away parts of the floor allowing visual access or sight lines in the center or along walls. Another approach is to locate more destination-oriented merchandise and departments, or areas requiring more intimacy, or service on the other levels. Balconies are extremely exciting and can be quite an interesting focal point. If railings are used allowing sight through, remember not to clutter with fixtures or merchandise along the railings. Make the view interesting and possibly very dramatic.

At times ceiling treatments can be used to direct traffic flow through a space. Variations in materials also add interest. If the ceiling is existing, a suspended grid or other materials can be introduced to make certain areas more intimate than others.

If the store is located where skylights can be considered, this type of installation always gets attention and is different than most ceiling and roof treatments.

We have covered suspended and drywall ceilings but one other alternative is to allow the entire or portions of the existing structural wood or steel to be exposed. Keep in mind, however, that this also allows viewing of all electrical, HVAC, sprinkler heads and other mechanical support elements.

FINISHES AND MATERIALS

Finishes and materials should be well thought through for the storefront and interior spaces. These items strongly influence the overall feeling and mood of the store.

The one thing to remember is that colors and textures are very personal and will vary greatly from one customer to another. Colors can attract or they can be offensive.

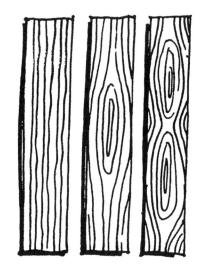

When designing a store, make a list of the different items that will receive finishes and the materials involved. A typical list may include:
• Flooring
• Walls
• Ceiling
• Floor and wall display fixtures (Note that in this area, multiple finishes and combinations of materials are typically used)
• Lighting fixtures
• Architectural elements such as railings, steps, wood trimming, cove base, reducer strips and hardware

Storefront materials should always be very durable and maintenance never an issue. Hard surfaces such as the following are common, but be creative and innovative:
• Marble, granite, and other natural stone elements
• Stained or natural finished hardwoods
• Metals
• Brick
• Solid-core plastic laminates or composition materials such as Corian® or Avonite®
• Lacquered surfaces with adequate layers or coats

The colors introduced can be subtle or loud, light or dark, contrasting or complementary. Think through the color and material palette. Sometimes scale models or design sketches are done in color to properly study the applications and understand the finished product.

When it comes to retail store design there is a need to make a statement in order to stand out from others. This can be achieved through the use of exciting floor coverings. In fact, combinations of colors and materials get a lot of positive attention.

There are several ways to differentiate parts of the store or define traffic aisles with different materials. Keep in mind that some areas will receive greater wear and traffic. Application for hard surfaces such as vinyl flooring, tiles, ceramics or natural stones, wood planking and even carpet, designed to accept the wear and offering soil-hiding colorations or patterns, is appropriate. At store entrances or in front of service counters, patterns and even store logos are great focal points. At the same time, depending on the overall store image, sealed, stained or painted concrete works just fine.

Even when costs are an issue for flooring budgets, accent colors in tile areas do not have to cost any more. Carpets of different colors can be installed in stripes or bands.

One important point: When you clearly define aisles with different colors and/or materials, they clearly define spaces. If movement of departments due to growth or reduction is necessary, this can limit the progress. If you do define aisles, make sure that they are the right width. Aisles should allow for passage of at least two persons if the aisles are main aisles and a minimum of 3' if they are secondary.

When buying carpet, make sure that you are discussing only commercial grade quality and not residential. The same applies to all flooring materials. Some salespersons at carpet stores, even national chains, are not educated to understand the difference. I typically specify 100% banded nylon, solution dyed with a face weight of 26-32 ounces as a minimum. Both styles, cut piles and level loops, can be used, even in combinations for interest. Commercial carpet sales representatives will only work through distributors or design firms. They do not sell directly to retail end users. In working with a store designer, ask about the purchase of materials. They do not typically mark-up as much as when dealing with installers or even distributors.

Remember to not only think about the colors, but also textures involved with floor coverings.

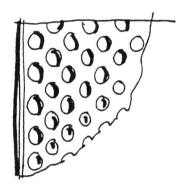

½" ALTERNATING PERF METAL PATTERN

Wall finishes require attention and not simply picking out paint colors and applying throughout. Variety in colors and tones creates retail excitement.

Take for example a different paint color used in focal areas throughout the store. This will reinforce that is special area compared to the standard wall merchandised portions of the store. Keep in mind that paint is very inexpensive and change is easily completed. Painting is something that most store owners can complete on their own.

For extra effect, apply two or more different paint colors and apply by means of sponges, rags, newspapers rollers or brushes. If you check with local paint resources, they will typically have sample display boards in their showroom and stores to review different examples. If working with a painter, ask if they are capable of custom and special finishes. it is actually possible to achieve the looks of woodgrain, marble and stone.

EXPANDED METAL PANEL

Wallcoverings also make areas special and differentiate from other finishes. If using this material, make sure that it is durable. Regular papers are not recommended. Some have a vinyl coating. Of course, there are many different types of solid vinyls available in literally thousands of colors and textures. There are also wallcoverings that come in basic white or beige that can be installed and painted a color from the store itself.

In general, put some thought into and be creative about wall finishes. Especially the exposed surfaces.

If heavy traffic is an issue, consider installing plastic laminate, solid sheet vinyl or even metal panels to walls. Furthermore, you may want to consider moldings and trims horizontally on walls or on corners. There are many options available in rubber, metal and wood.

Fixture finishes should always be a high priority in the retail store. There are many different options available as standard offerings. Most display fixture manufacturers in wood, metal and glass also have created their own custom finishes differentiating themselves from others. Durability is the major concern when discussing fixture finishes since they are exposed to constant customer use and abuse. No matter how hard you try to make them impervious to damage, it is nearly impossible to prevent damage over time.

When ceilings are lay-in tile systems, review the available choices from a local supplier. You will find that there are many textures, materials and colorations available beyond standard white 2' x 4' versions. Remember that you can simply install different tiles in certain areas for added interest and do not have to effect the entire ceiling area.

Lastly, consider the finishes and colorations of your lighting fixtures for compatibility to the overall design direction.

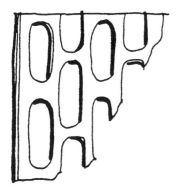

ELONGATED ALTERNATING
PERF. MTL. PATTERN.
(SIMILAR TO SAFETY
STEP DESIGNS)

STOREFRONT

In most centers the landlord has tight design control over the storefront. While this is important from the standpoint of cohesive mall design direction, it doesn't always allow for greatest contrast among the stores.

All storefronts, regardless of design direction, are the dividers between the outside and interior. A storefront conveys the first impression and is how passersby evaluate the store. The storefront should always complement the store interior. The image message should be consistent.

Architecturally, the storefront can make a real design statement with the use of materials and dimension. Pop-outs and recessed areas help to create excitement and interest. Sometimes design can even be a series of individual elements such as columns or archways in front of or behind the majority of the storefront or lease line.

Extension past the lease line is determined by the landlord's design codes. However, when allowed, this can be achieved by entire or partial front bump-outs, or by extension of the bulkhead or sign-band. Projections certainly add interest and variety to a center.

The percentages of solid versus glass materials incorporated into the design can provide great contrast. It's also the means of determining size(s) of display windows. These two factors must also be supported by the actual entrance opening. The three parts must work as a whole and culminate in a single design direction or statement.

The storefront entrance also depicts a value message. Typically the lower the price point, the wider the entrance. However, this isn't always true. Since design is also a major control factor, this rule is sometimes bent. There are many types of storefront closures to consider (either solid, glass or metal):

- Overhead and side sliding grilles
- Swinging doors
- Side sliding doors
- Vestibules
- Revolving doors
- Single or double doors

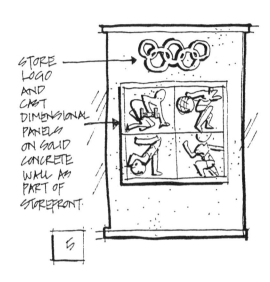

STORE LOGO AND CAST DIMENSIONAL PANELS ON SOLID CONCRETE WALL AS PART OF STOREFRONT

Storefront signage is also closely related to the overall design concept. Elements that make each sign unique are:

• Size
• Character
• Typography
• Composition
• Illumination
• Height
• Color
• Materials

Not all signs are mounted to the exterior of a store. As part of the design concept, some signs are installed behind the storefront within the first eight feet — the area known as the design control zone. This approach usually is entertained when the entire storefront is comprised of glass.

There are also opportunities to use blade signs extended out from the storefront or ceiling mounted to bottoms of overhangs. This increases the exposure of the store adding architectural and graphic dimension.

Many landlords do not allow the application of credit card signs, store hours, sale signs, etc., to the interior or exterior of the storefront. Such signs detract from the overall merchandise statement and architecture. Even promotional signage is controlled and exceptions permitted only (in writing) by the landlord. Again, while this may seem like tight control, it's necessary to ensure a uniform and planned image for the overall center.

When involved with store design in strip centers versus enclosed malls, the amount of personality is usually even less. This is because the local codes control the exterior architectural elements and signage style, size and color at times. Note that this situation often allows for an added under canopy sign introduction, perpendicular to the storefront. Some centers will allow the repeat of store name in smaller scale, vinyl sticker applied to the interior of front glass windows.

Freestanding street stores often have some of the best opportunities for individualism. This is due to the fact that they are separate from other factors or stores requiring unified design direction.

When necessary, storefront awnings should be considered for protection from inclement weather or even sun control. There are various types of moveable styles available. Yet the proven most durable material still seems to be metal versus canvas.

Illuminated awnings not only attract at night but can serve as the actual signage area. This approach also illuminates the storefront below.

Remember that in some situations, you should remodel the exterior of your storefront or at least update it. This will attract not only the existing customers but also indicates something new to others. This is the first item the customer sees.

OVERHEAD WITH
RECESSED LIGHT
FIXTURES TO HIGHLIGHT
STORENAME ABOVE
ENTRANCE

FULL ROUND CONCRETE
COLUMNS TO EACH SIDE
OF ENTRANCE.

RECESSED LIGHTS

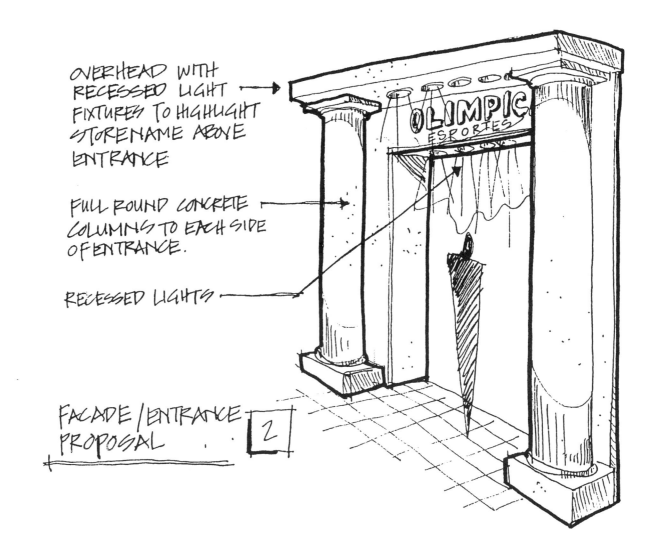

FACADE / ENTRANCE
PROPOSAL   2

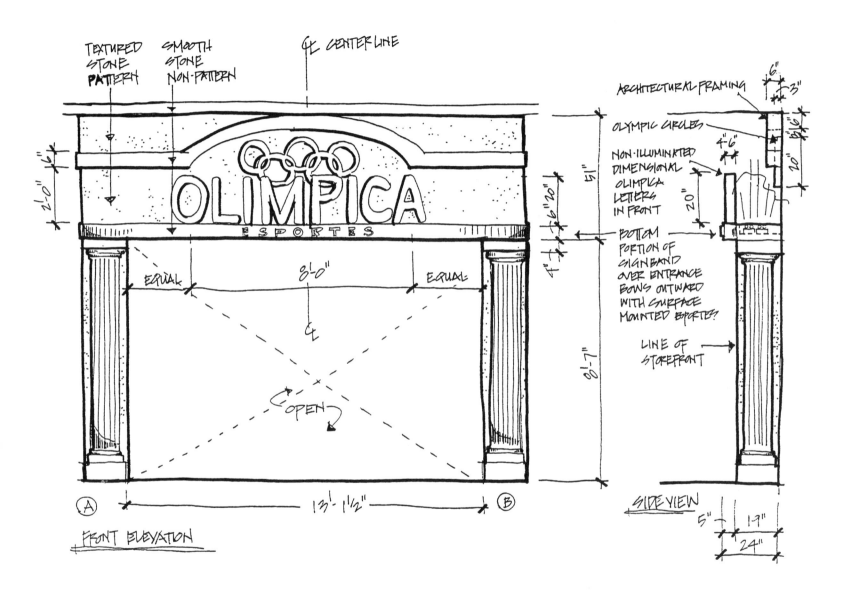

TEXTURED STONE PATTERN

SMOOTH STONE NON-PATTERN

℄ CENTER LINE

ARCHITECTURAL FRAMING

6"
3"

OLYMPIC CIRCLES

NON-ILLUMINATED DIMENSIONAL OLIMPICA LETTERS IN FRONT

4" 6"

20"

0'-6"

20"

OLIMPICA
ESPORTES

2'-0"
6"

5'-1"

6'-0"
10"

1"

BOTTOM PORTION OF SIGNBAND OVER ENTRANCE BOWS OUTWARD WITH SURFACE MOUNTED ESPORTES?

EQUAL

8'-0"

℄

EQUAL

LINE OF STOREFRONT

OPEN

0'-7"

Ⓐ

13'-1½"

Ⓑ

FRONT ELEVATION

SIDE VIEW

5"

17"

24"

94

STOREFRONT WINDOWS

The popularity of storefront windows comes and goes. Is it determined by trends within the display industry, actual merchandising requirements or cost? Hopefully you did not pick the last choice.

① ▶ DRAPED MATERIAL, LARGE FROSTED BOTTLE SILHOUETTE, SAND BLASTED LOGO, SMALL DISPLAY TABLES AND BOTTLES.

I saw a billboard on the highway that displayed a priceless message:
"IT DOESN'T COST, IT PAYS."

The state lotteries coined a phrase:
"IF YOU DON'T PLAY, IT WON'T PAY."

And for as long as memory, we've all said from one time to another, for one reason or another:

"YOU GET WHAT YOU PAY FOR."

"YOU GET OUT OF IT WHAT YOU PUT INTO IT."

"IT'S NOT AN EXPENSE, IT'S AN INVESTMENT IN THE FUTURE."

"DON'T BE PENNY-WISE AND DOLLAR FOOLISH."

Now don't get the wrong impression here. It's not that you must spend a lot of money with regard to windows. Some of the best display statements actually cost very little. Sometimes the most important investment is the time spent — it can be priceless. Again, why rush through the planning and decision-making process? You need to give adequate thought, time, expense and proper execution.

Just make sure that the window statement supports and is consistent with the interior image.

In some cases the backs of the display windows are closed or solid. This is often done for several reasons:

• The windows may be part of the stock room area and not adjacent to or on the sales floor
• The sales floor may need to maximize the opportunity for vertical merchandising and wall space
• Landlord design criteria may dictate certain percentages of open versus solid wall areas within the storefront
• The windows may be existing and you simply have to compensate for them since the option of removal doesn't come into play

Considering your limitations, plan the display statement. Keep consistent with the interior direction, and don't feel the need to fill every little square inch of space.

The approach may be to use color as part of the window statement. This doesn't have to be permanent. Paint is temporary since it can be easily changed. Large pieces of paper or panels are easy to work with as well.

The use of display panels, shelving units or even pieces of furniture can be very dramatic and powerful. These elements also tend to limit re-arrangement options and quell the desire of a sales associate to use all of the space.

Remember, when you plan a window display, make sure you take the time to define the directions in an easy-to-understand format so that the person responsible for execution is comfortable with the responsibility of setting the display window accordingly. Make them a part of the final decision if possible. This can be a TEAM project.

FLORAL TILE PATTERN BACKGROUND

CASMIR

② ▶ SILKSCREEN ON DRAPERY HOLDER WITH OVERSIZED BOTTLE. VINYL LETTERS ON GLASS IN FOREGROUND WITH MARKETING MESSAGE, I.E. "THE ENCHANTMENT OF THE MOMENT..."

MARKETING MESSAGES ON BACKDROP

...the enchantment
of the moment...
...the sense of eternity
in the face of time...

CHOPARD CASMIR

③ ▷ LARGE VASE/URN WITH ROSES, GOLD
BRAIDED ROPING, SINGLE LEG PEDESTAL
DISPLAYER.

Execution of the window installation is critical to the overall completed product.

Far too often a great idea comes off the drawing board and dies due to improper dedication to the actual installation. Keep in mind the people who will actually install the display. Establish for them the display elements and tools required and provide step-by-step instructions to follow.

Not every store or company has someone on staff responsible for the project. If you don't, then you must plan accordingly. You can hire local talent if necessary. Such talent is readily available in every market. They work in department and specialty store chains, design offices or other creative environments in every community. Most of these professionals are available for freelance work and welcome the chance. The store can contract for monthly services, quarterly or seasonally, depending on the need. The plan may be to utilize a professional to train or work with a permanent associate in the store.

It is not uncommon to hire a professional visual merchandiser from out of state to develop a yearly program that is installed by that professional or store associates.

Make sure that when working with a designer or visual merchandiser that the communication in the relationship is completely open and free flowing. The two will need to work as a team. The store owner will need to define certain directions such as: the defined store image and customer profile; merchandise assortment today and in the future; growth potential; and, of course, the budget, timing and action schedule. Establish the design fees for the services up front and work with a contract.

There are many rules of thumb to follow in regards to the displaying of merchandise or use of storefront display windows. The important thing to remember is to be able to control what you design or have designed for you. It's just as important to be able to maintain the displays.

Remember one important fact: The window display is the first message you are sending to regular and potential customers. Therefore, you must carefully plan the merchandise and how it is presented. It's not unlike how you get dressed each day. You carefully coordinate the clothes you want to wear and the manner in which you style your hair or apply make-up. Your storefront window displays should be given the same level of primary importance.

The recommended approach to window design is to keep the statement focused, controlled and balanced, and allow room for the customer to see beyond the "window dressing" into the store if possible. The wrong approach is to fill the window area with everything you can find. Since window displays are changed regularly, everything will have its scheduled appearance in the window.

Another negative to cramming everything into the windows is that there may be less of an incentive or reason for the customer to enter your store. Window displays need only represent the quality and personality of your store's merchandise directions. And, it isn't always recommended to display price tags. Although it's appropriate during sale or clearance events, it is not on a daily basis. Let the customers enter the store before they decide if the price is acceptable or possibly more than they prefer to spend.

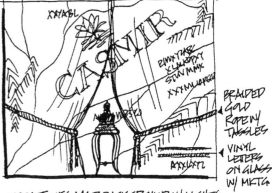

④ ▸ SEPIA TONES MAP BACKGROUND. W/ LIGHTS OPTIONAL SHEER DRAPES IN FRONT PARTIALLY OPEN TO EXPOSE AND FRAME SINGLE TABLE.

+ WINDOWS

The defined window display direction should not be rigid — just controlled and consistent. It too should be open to change and fresh approaches.

The word that best applies here is "options."
The best phrase is "always entertain options."

The balance established in the window displays should change from one setting to the next. This keeps your windows exciting and different.

YOU DON'T WANT TO BE PREDICTABLE.

KEEP CUSTOMERS GUESSING.

KEEP THEM COMING BACK TO SEE WHAT EXCITING NEW STATEMENT THE STORE IS MAKING THIS WEEK OR MONTH.

MAKE A STATEMENT, SHOW SOME PERSONALITY.

RETAIL IS ENTERTAINMENT AND THEATRE.

TAKE A RISK WITH CHANGE.

The illustrations on the left of this page show several options of how to use the window areas differently. Yet, each option still maintains the balance of solid image/mass to stop the eye and open areas to view beyond into the store.

Look at your competition and make notes on what they are doing, both right and wrong. Learn from their examples and mistakes. Take a good idea, modify it to fit your marketing image and improve upon it for your store.

Take photos of windows that you liked, clip magazine ads, read and subscribe to industry magazines. There are many great books available for application and reference.

⑤ LARGE (± 36" DIAM) ROSE BUDS, TONE ON TONE WITH WINDOW, PEDESTAL FRONT RIGHT W/ PRODUCT.

With a balanced window display, the passerby/potential customer, can quickly identify the particular items in the window but also view into the store. Allowing the customer to view into the store actually invites them past the window. The purpose of the window display is to simply get their attention and stop them. You may consider it an invitation to come into the store and examine the rest of your wonderful assorted merchandise. This is the reason to place emphasis on the interior focal points.

Besides the storefront window displays, the area considered to be even more important is the display/merchandising opportunity just inside the entrance. The point is, when the customer approaches this display for closer examination, she is inside your store.

Remember, you want to get their attention, stop them and bring them into your store. At that point, you have increased the possibility of actually generating a sales opportunity.

The display floor focal just inside should be more dramatic than the windows. In some cases depending on the actual size of your store, the center display may be the only statement that can be made. In a situation like this, the secondary display areas are located on the walls at the front lease line.

Use the generic storefront elevation on the next page to indicate your store's image today. Show what customers see as they stand in front of your store from across the mall or in the parking lot. Show the areas that allow the customer to see into the store clearly without looking through a fixture or wall of merchandise.

Then use the example window on the next page to indicate a different approach, improving or simply showing options.

FRONT WINDOW CUT-OUT FRAMING MUSEUM DISPLAY.

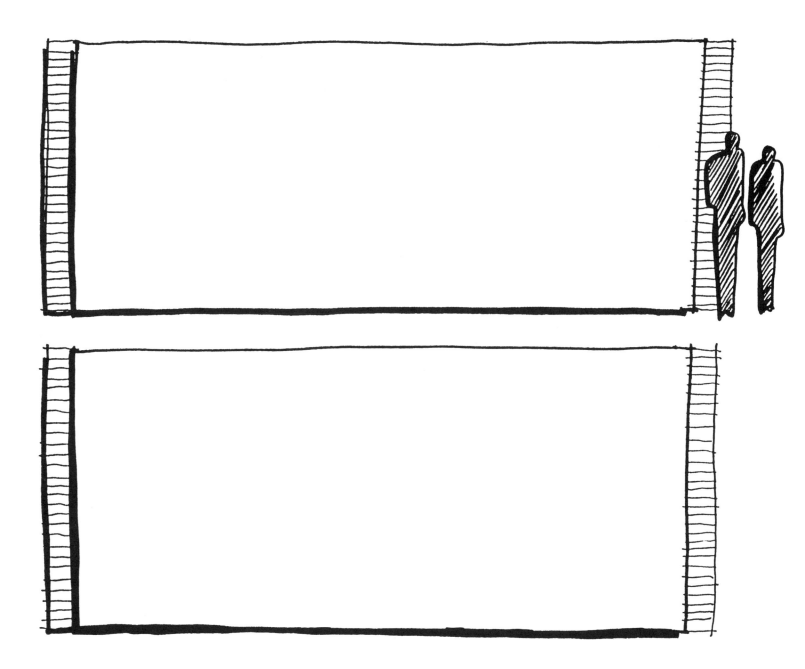

DESIGN FOR THE SENSES

SIGHT, SOUND, TOUCH, SMELL AND TASTE

A favorable and memorable shopping experience is best achieved when it stimulates all of the senses. Messages can be either obvious or subliminal, but should balance and complement each other. For example, you might have music playing throughout the store, but strategically place other sensory zones within the store for customers to discover themselves. And that sense of DISCOVERY is something important, too.

Sight is stimulated through visual excitement, merchandising and signage applications. It involves the use of flat or dimensional items intended to attract and complement the store image.

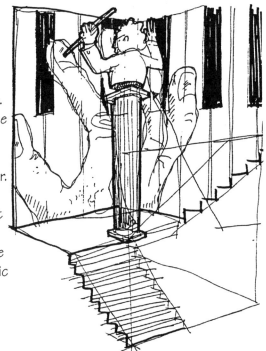

Sound, like every aspect of the store design, must complement your image and customer. Noise levels within a space should be positive reinforcement. It may be that different sounds are introduced at different areas of the store at the various levels. The easiest way to obtain sound is to turn on a radio. However, commercial radio stations play commercials, which may not be exactly what you want. Tapes and compact discs can be used to avoid commercial interruptions and dee-jays. Remember, though, recorded music is subject to regulations and royalties. Your area may not strictly enforce these rules, but be prepared for a visit someday.

Touch can also be referred to and accomplished through texture of materials. The application can be on floors, walls, fixtures or even ceilings.

Smell is a "touchy" and very personal subject. Each person responds to certain aromas differently. Merchandise such as candles, potpourri, incense, food items, candies, colognes, perfumes and materials such as leather, mean the merchandising will involve smell. Plan accordingly depending on your merchandise selections.

Last comes the sense of discovery. In many store situations, the customer can easily scan the entire store or a major portion of it. There are two basic assumptions that can be applied. The first, and most often common approach, is to have the store wide open so that the customer can see and discover easily.

The second approach, and one that is acceptable if understood, is to allow partial vision into stores. What is open to view tends to have greater importance and focal impact. Partial viewing doesn't allow customers to quickly and wrongly determine that they understand everything being offered in the store, and walk out. Partial views send a message that the customer may be missing something and should walk the store just to verify.

There are many ways to introduce partial view. The most common is to use walls in the center of the store or partitions perpendicular to perimeter walls between departments. Although some of these walls are part of fixture systems that can be dismantled, they require multiple persons and are usually not time efficient compared to all of the other retail store demands. The next option is to introduce large oversized fixture walls that incorporate heavy duty casters within the base of the unit. This allows for movement with less disruption.

Visual excitement or merchandising treatments can also be incorporated alone or with other options to stop the eye. Strategically located focal areas on top of freestanding floor fixtures can be easily installed and even changed. The use of ceiling-suspended banners can work, but be careful about the quality of the message you are sending. Make sure that the graphic or fabric panel supports a focal point below and may even be an integral part of the message. The great thing about fabric as wall partitions is the texture and softness that it introduces or complements to other parts of the store.

Keep in mind that the use of vertical display surfaces increases both merchandise capacity and focal opportunities. So often the size of a particular department expands past the desired floor square footage, based on merchandise space. Height helps to correct the situation. Multiple height fixtures even add increased visual excitement since from a distance the customer can see multiple merchandise or visual focal point offerings. Always try to incorporate height, low to high, front to back or middle to side. This defines a particular area. However, remember that high walls strategically located in the center of large areas or between departments introduce the sense of discovery, and departmentalization.

SECURITY

The security elements required for each store are handled differently depending on the type and price points of the merchandise. Not all stores need go to the farthest extreme.

There are however a few basic preventive approaches that can be taken to reduce or prevent shoplifting.

• Install security cameras and monitors. Prop or false rotating cameras that require electrical connections and those that don't are both available.

• Domes in the ceiling are used typically to enclose cameras so shoplifters can't detect which direction the camera is looking. Domes can be used without the cameras and even as mirrors.

• Wall mounted mirrors allow for viewing into hidden areas, corners or aisles.

• Two-way wall mirrors or lay-in ceiling panels are designed to house cameras or actual loss-prevention personnel.

• Motion detectors or light beams at the entrance to a store usually ring a bell or chime identifying that someone just entered or left the store.

• Electronic alarm systems can be placed to the sides or above the store entrance, detecting when a piece of merchandise with a specific device attached passes through. When used, please make sure that the tag is removed at the time of purchase because it can be very embarrassing for a customer to set off the alarm by mistake.

• Some stores install the trappings of the electronic door passage alarms without the system attached. Potential shoplifters get the visual message without the sales staff having to keep track of garment tags.

• Grilles are used alone or in conjunction with doors and windows for added protection in high risk areas.

• Some stores may choose to hire actual guards either in uniform or plain clothes to stand at the entrance or wander through the store.

• If you feel you must use a sign that reads: "Shoplifting is a crime" or "Shoplifters will be prosecuted," then be tasteful and place it in a frame at the very least. These signs can be intimidating and insulting at the same time.

Again, depending on the types of merchandise, you may want to use lockable glass display cases. This allows the store to display an assortment of higher priced or small items safely. However, even glass showcases at times require alarms and cameras.

One thing to remember is that when using cases, because customers cannot wait on themselves and review the items, customer service is very important. A customer shouldn't have to wait too long to be acknowledged and assisted. Some stores use a ticket/number system so customers know approximately when they will be helped.

And of course the oldest type ever used is the bell or chime attached to the door sounding tones when the door is moved.

You may want to have signals in your store either verbal or by hand that notify when there is someone who requires watching. Large department stores sometimes have bells that signal security to go to a specific area within the store.

Thinking about security should really start when deciding upon what type of merchandise will be carried and the planning of the store. Store designers and owners can prevent losses based on location of store and the local demographics. Ask questions and request statistics from local law enforcement offices. Call the library and they can share facts and research findings with you.

Next, consider locations of specific departments or merchandise types within your store. Do not locate high-loss items near the front window, door or lease line. Position this merchandise where it can be regularly monitored, away from the front of the store.

When cases and locking devices are required, make sure you investigate the different types available before finalizing. You will find that some are more aesthetically appealing than others and some while they may look invincible, are not.

Try to keep open sight lines available from the service counter through the entire store as much as possible. Have sales associates on the floor walking around. Try to keep open

Sample store plans

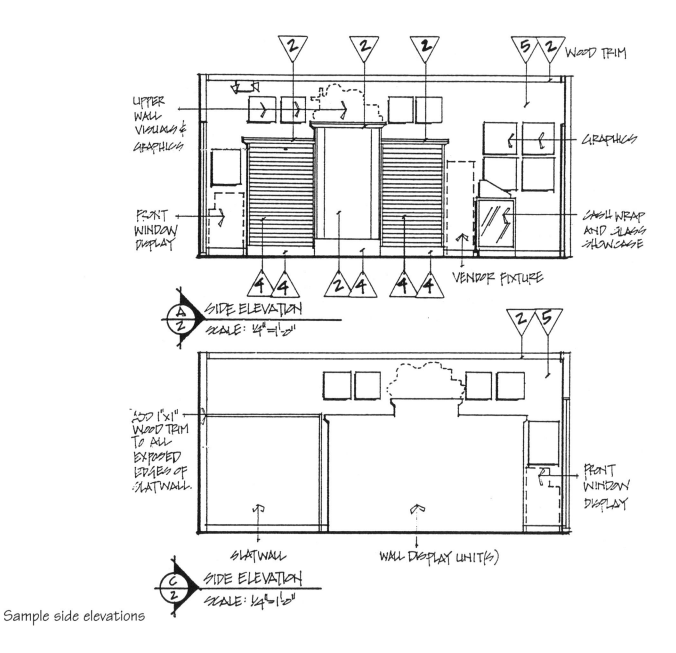

UPPER WALL VISUALS & GRAPHICS

WOOD TRIM

GRAPHICS

FRONT WINDOW DISPLAY

CASH WRAP AND GLASS SHOWCASE

VENDOR FIXTURE

SIDE ELEVATION
SCALE: ¼"=1'-0"

ADD 1"x1" WOOD TRIM TO ALL EXPOSED EDGES OF SLATWALL.

FRONT WINDOW DISPLAY

SLATWALL

WALL DISPLAY UNIT(S)

SIDE ELEVATION
SCALE: ¼"=1'-0"

Sample side elevations

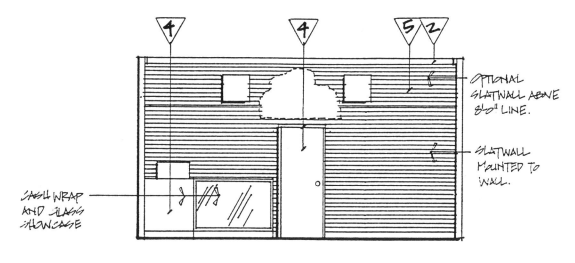

OPTIONAL
SLATWALL ABOVE
8'-0" LINE.

SLATWALL
MOUNTED TO
WALL.

CASH WRAP
AND GLASS
SHOWCASE

B/2 REAR ELEVATION
SCALE: 1/4" = 1'-0"

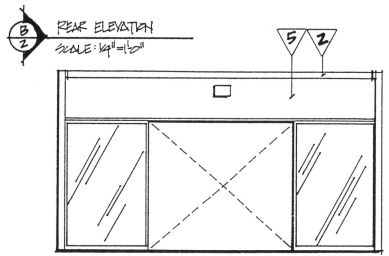

D/2 FRONT (INTERIOR) ELEVATION
SCALE: 1/4" = 1'-0"

Sample front and rear elevations

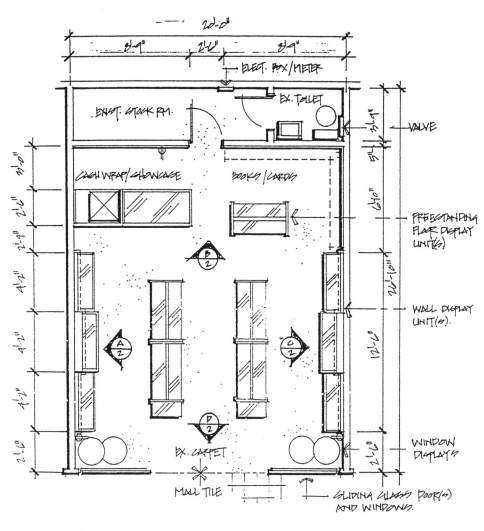

20'-0"

8'-9"   2'-6"   8'-9"

ELECT. BOX/METER

EX. TOILET

EXIST. STOCK RM.

CASH WRAP/SHOWCASE

BOOKS/CARDS

VALVE

3'-9"   5"

6'-0"

26'-10"

12'-0"

2'-6"

FREESTANDING
FLOOR DISPLAY
UNIT(S)

WALL DISPLAY
UNIT(S)

WINDOW
DISPLAYS

3'-0"   2'-6"   2'-6"   4'-2"   4'-2"   4'-2"   2'-6"

EX. CARPET

MALL TILE

SLIDING GLASS DOOR(S)
AND WINDOWS.

FIXTURE/FLOOR PLAN
SCALE: 1/4" = 1'-0"

➤ ALL DIMENSIONS TO BE VERIFIED
BY FIXTURE INSTALLER PRIOR
TO FINAL INSTALLATION AND
APPROVED BY OWNER.

Sample fixture floor plan

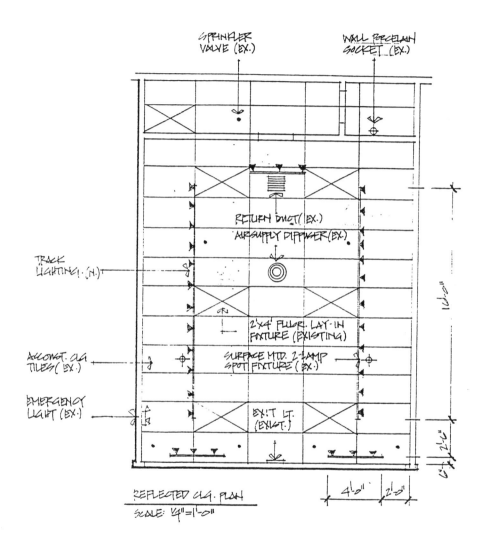

SPRINKLER VALVE (EX.)

WALL PORCELAIN SOCKET (EX.)

RETURN DUCT (EX.)

AIR SUPPLY DIFFUSER (EX.)

TRACK LIGHTING (N.)

2'X4' FLUOR. LAY-IN FIXTURE (EXISTING)

ACOUST. CLG. TILES (EX.)

SURFACE MTD. 2-LAMP SPOT FIXTURE (EX.)

EMERGENCY LIGHT (EX.)

EXIT LT. (EXIST.)

REFLECTED CLG. PLAN
SCALE: ¼"=1'-0"

4'-0" 2'-0"

Sample reflected ceiling plan

For more information on visual merchandising and store design, subscribe to:

Books on visual merchandising and store design available from ST Media Group International:

Aesthetics of Merchandising Presentation | Budget Guide to Retail Store Planning & Design
Complete Guide to Effective Jewelry Store Display | Feng Shui for Retailers | Retail Renovation
Retail Store Planning & Design Manual | Stores and Retail Spaces | Visual Merchandising
Visual Merchandising and Store Design Workbook

To subscribe, order books or request a complete catalog of related books and magazines, contact:

ST Media Group International Inc.
11262 Cornell Park Drive. | Cincinnati, Ohio 45242
p: 1.800.925.1110 or 513.421.2050
f: 513.421.5144 or 513.744.6999

e: books@stmediagroup.com
www.bookstore.stmediagroup.com (ST Books)
www.vmsd.com (*VMSD* Magazine)
www.irdconline.com (International Retail Design Conference)